RC
LYRICS
TRIVIA QUIZ BOOK

"featuring pop/rock stars
from the 1950s & 1960s"

--(pre-British Invasion)--

250 ROCK LYRICS QUESTIONS/
250 ROCK TITLES QUESTIONS

*an encyclopedia of rock & roll's
most memorable lyrics

in question/answer format*

by: Presley Love

Published by Hi-Lite Publishing Co.

Copyright © 2015, 2018 by:
Raymond Karelitz
Hi-Lite Publishing Company
Rock-&-Roll Test Prep Hawaii
P.O. Box 6071
Kaneohe, Hawaii 96744

email comments/corrections: <u>rocknrolltriviaquizbook.com</u>
(808) 261-6666

4ᵗʰ EDITION -- Updated Printing: 2019

note: though listed as Vol. 2—text is updated version of Vol. 1, which is no longer in print

Love, Presley
ROCK LYRICS & TITLES TRIVIA QUIZ BOOK (1955-1964)
(128 pages)

1. Rock-&-Roll Trivia Quiz Book   I. Love, Presley   II. Title: Rock and Roll

2. Music

COVER DESIGN: *Doug Behrens*

ISBN: 978-1523306053

Printed In The United States of America

A Magical Musical Tour Through the Past

Once you open this book, you will be transported back to the time of magical musical memories, a mosaic of music at your fingertips!

Browse through the streets where the '50s & '60s still rule. Test your rock trivia expertise — invite your friends to see who's the ROCK LYRIC KING!

Rock & Roll is here to stay, and now every memory-making word can be recalled whenever you feel like escaping to the past, groovin' where no person has gone before! Put on your oldies records, let their words of wisdom come alive for you, then sit back in ecstasy and let the good vibrations take you on a magic swirling ship headed on a collision course with the classics!

****

To be best prepared for this book, listen to lots of rock & roll — heavily energized with the King, Chuck Berry and Buddy Holly — and be sure not to forget the Shirelles, Crystals and Chubby Checker. For added flavor, locate the nearest jukebox at your favorite malt shop for even more Rock & Roll!

[caution: a limbo-stick can cause uncontrollable happiness, Daddio!]

text collection by: **Presley Love**
format/production by: Raymond Karelitz

The Legacy of Presley Love

In 1992, music-aficionado Presley Love compiled a vast treasure of rock & roll lyric-memoribilia, including songs from the earliest days of rock & roll up through the late '80s. This musical quiz-format collection lay dormant except for the release of a single volume which contained 400 questions. The original book — printed in 1992 — became, over the years, an Amazon.com favorite, with very positive response from those who loved the book for its "party-flavor" appeal.

In 2014, the entire vault of Presley Love's music-lyric memoribilia was located in a storage locker — containing his collection of lyric-questions and trivia questions in quiz format! After four years of diligent compiling and organizing, the entire Presley Love collection of rock lyrics, rock titles and rock group trivia is now available in quiz-format!

We are proud to unveil *ROCK LYRICS & TITLES TRIVIA QUIZ BOOK* (1955-1964), a special volume of this rare and collectible series. We sincerely hope you enjoy these fabulous rock-favorites in quiz-format from Presley Love's truly incredible treasure trove of rock & roll memories 1955-1989 collection!

ROCK LYRICS QUESTIONS

If you're brave enough to test your skills,
here's a simple SCORING CHART:

(questions are worth 1 point each — "Harder Questions"
are worth 2 points each . . . If you are able to correctly
answer the question without referring to the three
choices, you receive twice the point value!)

If you score . . .

25+ Points: You probably STILL think it's 1959!
(Check your wardrobe!)

20–24: You probably paid more attention to
rock & roll than books & school!
(Check your report card!)

15–19: There's a lot of rock & roll memories
in your blood!
*(But maybe it's time to buy
a few more rock & roll LPs!)*

10–14: Don't you wish you'd listened more closely
to rock & roll ?!
(It's never too late to be hip!)

0–9: Where were YOU when rock began to rule ?!
*(Time to get experienced —
run to your music store now!!!)*

(note: all answers are derived from lyrics within the song)

1. In *Surrender,* what does Elvis Presley say happens to his heart when you and he kiss ?
   - a. it's on fire
   - b. it wanders
   - c. it has a mind of its own

***

2. In *Gee Whiz (Look at His Eyes),* what does Carla Thomas say about his eyes ?
   - a. they hypnotize
   - b. they hide his secret sighs
   - c. they are marble-size

***

3. When you *Catch a Falling Star,* what does Perry Como say you should do with it ?
   - a. give it to a stranger
   - b. put it in your pocket
   - c. let it light up your life

***

4. In *Banana Boat (Day-O),* what does Harry Belafonte see that makes him want to go home ?
   - a. rain
   - b. daylight
   - c. a lackluster future

***

5. What are the Four Lads *Standing On the Corner* doing ?
   - a. watching all the girls go by
   - b. waiting for the light to change
   - c. leaning on a lamp post

6. In *Goodnight Sweetheart,* what do the Spaniels wish for tomorrow to be for you ?

      a. sunny and bright

      b. snowy and white

      c. as dark as the night

****

7. What do the Dell Vikings want the *Whispering Bells* to do ?

      a. speak more loudly

      b. share their secret with them

      c. bring their baby back to them

****

8. In *All the Way,* if love is real, how deep does Frank Sinatra say it goes ?

      a. deeper than the deep–blue sea

      b. as deep as your soul

      c. not as deep as your heart

****

9. In *Sorry (I Ran All the Way Home),* what didn't the Impalas mean to do ?

      a. be late to their first date

      b. miss the bus

      c. make you cry

****

10. What was Marty Robbins' only chance after his gunfight in *El Paso* ?

      a. to fight the law

      b. to lay down and die

      c. to run

11. In *Rock & Roll Is Here to Stay*, what do Danny & the Juniors say will become of rock & roll ?
    a. it'll soon change to rap and soul
    b. it'll go down in history
    c. it'll make the world a better place for you and me

****

12. In *Believe What You Say*, what does Ricky Nelson know for sure ?
    a. that you're going steady with nobody else
    b. that you've been lying to him
    c. that he's never met another girl like you before

****

13. In *My Heart Has a Mine of Its Own*, what did Connie Francis tell her heart ?
    a. not to believe all the lies
    b. that her love with you could never be
    c. not to beat so loud when you are near

****

14. Even though in *Baby It's You* it doesn't matter what others say — the Shirelles will love you anyway — what do the others call you ?
    a. a playboy
    b. a loser
    c. a cheat

****

15. In *To Know Him Is To Love Him*, what do the Teddy Bears' friends say will happen ?
    a. he'll leave them one day alone and broken-hearted
    b. their love will continue to grow throughout eternity
    c. there will come a day when they'll walk alongside of him

16. What does Little Richard want *Lucille* to satisfy ?
>   a. his appetite
>   b. his heart
>   c. his suspicions

****

17. In *Sh-Boom,* if you told the Crew–Cuts that they're the only one that you love, life for them could be a _____.
>   a. gas
>   b. ball
>   c. dream

****

18. When does Lesley Gore say that *Sunshine, Lollipops & Rainbows* are sure to come your way?
>   a. when you're in love
>   b. when you're at the county fair
>   c. when you're young

****

19. In *Sealed With a Kiss,* for what duration of time will Brian Hyland not be seeing you ?
>   a. for the rest of his life
>   b. for a week
>   c. for the summer

****

20. In *Danke Shoen,* what does Wayne Newton thank you for ?
>   a. all the joy and pain
>   b. being there for him
>   c. visiting him in Las Vegas

HARDER QUESTIONS: Worth 2 points each — 4 points if you can answer the question without the three choices !

****

1. According to Jane Morgan, what happened as a result of her *Fascination* with you ?

       a. it turned a passing glance into love

       b. it upset her life completely

       c. it soon became an obsession

****

2. Where does Steve Lawrence hear *Footsteps* ?

       a. in his mind

       b. down the hall

       c. on the lawn

****

3. Because the Clovers had so much fun after taking *Love Potion Number Nine,* what do they now wonder about ?

       a. Where will their love go from there?

       b. What will happen with Love Potion number ten?

       c. Is there a cure for the feeling they have?

****

4. According to Harvey & the Moonglows, what is the first of the *Ten Commandments of Love* ?

       a. thou shalt not steal

       b. thou shalt never love another

       c. thou shalt not doubt her love for you

****

5. Tommy Dee says that the *Three Stars* are for lovers, for wishing on, and for the _____.

       a. blessed

       b. dreamers

       c. lonely

ANSWERS

****

1. a. it's on fire
2. a. they hypnotize
3. b. put it in your pocket
4. b. daylight
5. a. watching all the girls go by
6. a. sunny and bright
7. c. bring their baby back to them
8. a. deeper than the deep-blue sea
9. c. make you cry
10. c. to run
11. b. it'll go down in history
12. a. that you're going steady with nobody else
13. b. that her love with you could never be
14. c. a cheat
15. c. there will come a day when they'll walk alongside of him
16. b. his heart
17. c. dream
18. a. when you're in love
19. c. for the summer
20. a. all the joy and pain

****

HARDER QUESTIONS--Answers

1. a. it turned a passing glance into love
2. b. down the hall
3. b. What will happen with Love Potion number ten?
4. b. thou shalt never love another
5. c. lonely

1. In *Do You Love Me,* why weren't the Contours loved ?

        a. they had an attitude
        b. they couldn't dance
        c. nobody else cared

****

2. What happened *One Summer Night* with the Danleers ?

        a. they were arrested
        b. they fell in love
        c. they stayed out too late with you

****

3. In Bobby Vinton's *Blue Velvet,* what was bluer than velvet ?

        a. her eyes
        b. his loneliness
        c.   the evening sky

****

4. In *Chances Are,* Johnny Mathis says that if you think he loves you, how accurate is your hunch ?

        a. it's not for him to say
        b. chances are awfully good
        c. it's an even chance

****

5. As long as Ben E. King knows you'll *Stand By Me,* what cataclysmic event still won't cause him to shed a tear ?

        a. if a riot should tear his town apart
        b. if his whole world were to shatter
        c. if the mountains should crumble to the sea

6. Why is it that the Serendipity Singers plead *Don't Let The Rain Come Down* ?

> a. because their roof has a hole in it
> b. because they're not insured
> c. because they want to cry alone

****

7. Because Eddie Cochran has a bad case of the *Summertime Blues,* how long does he want to take off from work to go on a vacation ?

> a. the entire summer
> b. two months
> c. two weeks

****

8. In *Whole Lotta Shakin' Goin' On,* what does Jerry Lee Lewis say they have in the barn ?

> a. a hay loft
> b. chicken
> c. lots of sheep

****

9. According to Shep & the Limelites, how long is it that *Daddy's Home* ?

> a. to stay
> b. for a week
> c. until the next teardrop falls

****

10. In *Breaking Up Is Hard to Do,* what does Neil Sedaka wish he were doing instead ?

> a. going to the party with someone else
> b. loving you
> c. making up

11. In *Rhythm of the Rain,* what has happened to the only girl the Cascades care about ?
- a. she's getting married
- b. she's gone away
- c. she's gotten hooked on drugs

****

12. What do the Four Seasons advise *Dawn* to think about before she decides to go out with them ?
- a. if they can really provide a happy home for her
- b. where they plan to go out tonight
- c. what the future would be if she stayed with them

****

13. What kind of *Chains* are the Cookies locked up in ?
- a. iron chains
- b. chains of fear
- c. chains of love

****

14. In *Little Town Flirt,* why does Del Shannon say that your heart had better be strong ?
- a. because she's a real hot lover
- b. because she'll love you forever and a day
- c. because you can hurt fooling around with her

****

15. In what street is it that the Dovells say *You Can't Sit Down* ?
- a. any street with music
- b. South Street
- c. Love Street

16. Dion, *The Wanderer,* is as happy as _____.

    a. a lark

    b. a clown

    c. Charlie Brown

****

17. In *Dedicated to the One I Love,* what do the Shirelles say is just before dawn ?

    a. the darkest hour

    b. the smell of morning dew

    c. the sound of the alarm bell

****

18. According to the Marcels, what did the *Blue Moon* see them doing ?

    a. standing alone

    b. smoking a reefer

    c. talking to the wind

****

19. According to Pat Boone, how did you react whenever he cried because the tide had erased his *Love Letters In the Sand* ?

    a. you held his hand

    b. you smiled tenderly

    c. you laughed

****

20. Where does Elvis Presley want to have his *Good Luck Charm* ?

    a. around his neck

    b. hanging on his arm

    c. waiting for him at home

HARDER QUESTIONS: Worth 2 points each — 4 points if you can answer the question without the three choices !

****

1. According to the Jarmels, what won't *A Little Bit of Soap* wash away ?

   a. their tears
   b. their guilt
   c. the blood

****

2. What is the name of the girl who was *Barefootin'* at Robert Parker's party ?

   a. Long Tall Sally
   b. Suzie Q
   c. Alice

****

3. In *Pretty Paper,* what does Roy Orbison say is near ?

   a. heartache
   b. your birthday
   c. Christmas

****

4. As you *Look in My Eyes,* what do the Chantels want you to do ?

   a. kiss them with emotion
   b. tell them you love them
   c. gaze and let them hypnotize

****

5. In *I Remember You,* what does Frank Ifield also remember with fondness ?

   a. the times you cried
   b. the beach he and you walked along
   c. a distant bell

ANSWERS

****

1. b. they couldn't dance
2. b. they fell in love
3. a. her eyes
4. b. chances are awfully good
5. c. if the mountains should crumble to the sea
6. a. because their roof has a hole in it
7. c. two weeks
8. b. chicken
9. a. to stay
10. c. making up
11. b. she's gone away
12. c. what the future would be if she stayed with them
13. c. chains of love
14. c. because you can hurt fooling around with her
15. b. South Street
16. b. a clown
17. a. the darkest hour
18. a. standing alone
19. c. you laughed
20. b. hanging on his arm

****

HARDER QUESTIONS--Answers

1. a. their tears
2. a. Long Tall Sally
3. c. Christmas
4. b. tell them you love them
5. c. a distant bell

1. What do the Four Preps say is the only thing that made them a *Big Man* ?
    - a. lies
    - b. you
    - c. small-minded friends

****

2. In *It's So Easy,* what do people tell Buddy Holly about love ?
    - a. that it's for fools
    - b. that it looks easier than it really is
    - c. that even a baby can fall in love

****

3. Ricky Nelson is *Stood Up* and _____.
    - a. broken-hearted
    - b. shot down
    - c. standing tall

****

4. How many *Silhouettes* did the Rays see on the shade ?
    - a. one
    - b. twelve
    - c. two

****

5. In *Such a Night,* Elvis Presley marvels over how she could _____.
    - a. fight
    - b. dance
    - c. kiss

6. According to Bobby Darin in *Mack the Knife,* what is the cement bag doing attached to the tug boat ?

 a. it's there to hide any trace of red
 b. it's there for the weight
 c. it's there to keep the boat from rocking

****

7. What is it that Sam Cooke wants you to *Bring It On Home to Me* ?

 a. your sweet lovin'
 b. your huggin' and your kissin'
 c. your paycheck

****

8. In *Nowhere to Run,* what are Martha & the Vandellas running from ?

 a. love
 b. the unknown
 c. heartbreak

****

9. What do the Platters say that *Only You* can do to the world ?

 a. give meaning to it
 b. make it bright
 c. make it go 'round

****

10. Who is the *Bird Dog* whom the Everly Brothers say is trying to steal their girl ?

 a. Stevie
 b. Joey
 c. Johnny

11. In *The End of the World,* what does Skeeter Davis wonder when she wakes up in the morning ?
    a. why everything is the same as it was
    b. why it's so dark outside
    c. if she can make it through the day

****

12. What does Jim Lowe ask *The Green Door* ?
    a. Is it true that green is the color of love?
    b. What's that secret you're keeping?
    c. What makes you so green?

****

13. In *Come Go With Me,* what do the Del–Vikings say you never give them ?
    a. a kiss
    b. a chance
    c. peace of mind

****

14. What is it that Elvis Presley wants to *Beg of You* ?
    a. not to break his heart
    b. to love him tonight
    c. to have the next dance with him

****

15. In *All Alone Am I,* what is the only thing that Brenda Lee hears ?
    a. the lonely beating of her heart
    b. the sound of people all around
    c. the words coming from your lips

16. In *Anna (Go With Him)*, what has Arthur Alexander been searching for all of his life ?
    a. a girl who loves him like he loves you
    b. a happiness that he had never known before
    c. a girl whose name is spelled the same backwards

****

17. What is Connie Stevens listing *Sixteen Reasons* to describe ?
    a. how beautiful you are
    b. why she loves you
    c. why she wants you out of her life

****

18. In *A Wonder Like You,* although Rick Nelson has traveled far away across the ocean blue to pyramids and snow-white mountains, what does he wish ?
    a. that he were back home
    b. that he had brought his camera along
    c. that you had been there with him

****

19. Why is it a *Tragedy* for the Fleetwoods ?
    a. because you're gone from them
    b. because they flunked history
    c. because they got caught kissing you in the hallway

****

20. Where does Ketty Lester say the *Love Letters* she receives comes straight from ?
    a. Santa Claus
    b. the post office
    c. your heart

HARDER QUESTIONS: Worth 2 points each — 4 points if you can answer the question without the three choices !

****

1. According to the Duprees in *My Own True Love,* what will no other lips or arms but yours do ?
   - a. protect them from harm's way
   - b. kiss and hug them
   - c. lead them through heaven's door

****

2. According to Dante & the Evergreens in *Time Machine,* who is the chick for them ?
   - a. you are
   - b. Cleopatra
   - c. Joan of Arc

****

3. When he's walking with you down *Primrose Lane,* what does Jerry Wallace say happens even in the rain ?
   - a. the sun shines
   - b. roses bloom
   - c. birds land on his shoulder

****

4. According to Johnny Preston, who jumped so high that he landed in the *Cradle of Love* ?
   - a. he did
   - b. Humpty Dumpty
   - c. Jack

****

5. In *Dreamy Eyes,* how does Johnny Tillotson first feel when he takes you home ?
   - a. so all alone
   - b. enchanted
   - c. like a little kid

ANSWERS

****

1. b. you
2. a. that it's for fools
3. a. broken-hearted
4. c. two
5. c. kiss
6. b. it's there for the weight
7. a. your sweet lovin'
8. c. heartbreak
9. b. make it bright
10. c. Johnny
11. a. why everything is the same as it was
12. b. What's that secret you're keeping?
13. b. a chance
14. a. not to break his heart
15. a. the lonely beating of her heart
16. a. a girl who loves him like he loves you
17. b. why she loves you
18. c. that you had been there with him
19. a. because you're gone from them
20. c. your heart

****

HARDER QUESTIONS--Answers

1. c. lead them through heaven's door
2. b. Cleopatra
3. b. roses bloom
4. c. Jack
5. a. so all alone

1. What do the Diamonds want their *Little Darlin'* to do ?
- a. hold their hand
- b. grow up
- c. call them on the telephone

****

2. In *It's Up to You*, what would Ricky Nelson give up everything he owns for ?
- a. a chance to be a teen idol again
- b. the chance to have you near
- c. the chance to start all over again

****

3. According to Bill Haley & His Comets in *Shake, Rattle & Roll,* even with your hair done up so nice, how are you deep inside ?
- a. cold as ice
- b. shy as a teenage queen
- c. playful like a cute tomboy

****

4. When will Fats Domino hurry to *My Blue Heaven* ?
- a. when lovin' is nigh
- b. when the whippoorwill calls
- c. when all his dreams turn to gold

****

5. In *Little Devil*, Neil Sedaka warns his mischievous friend that she's met her _____.
- a. future lover
- b. match
- c. Waterloo

6. In *Tiger,* Fabian says he's feeling stronger than

——————————.

      a. a mountain man

      b. a grizzly bear

      c. a saber-tooth

7. According to Jimmie Rodgers, what was made from a million trips to the *Honeycomb* ?

      a. a ton of honey

      b. his sweet love

      c. his baby's lips

8. In *I'm Hurtin',* what does Roy Orbison say happened to make the pain begin ?

      a. you walked away

      b. he tripped over a skateboard

      c. you kissed him in a way that only meant goodbye

9. In *Hello Stranger,* what does Barbara Lewis ask you not to do ?

      a. stare at her with a faraway look

      b. treat her like you did before

      c. give up without a fight

10. According to Carl Dobkins, Jr. in *My Heart Is an Open Book,* who does he love ?

      a. nobody

      b. everyone

      c. you

11. According to the Kingston Trio, where does *Tom Dooley* plan to be tomorrow ?

      a. in Tennessee

      b. hanging from an oak tree

      c. in his baby's arms

****

12. How many hours a day does Jimmy Jones work as the *Handy Man* ?

      a. eight to ten

      b. fourteen

      c. twenty-four

****

13. Why did Screamin' Jay Hawkins say *I Put a Spell on You* ?

      a. because you belong to him

      b. because you done him wrong

      c. because he's a magic man

****

14. In *She's a Fool,* what does Lesley Gore say that the girl doesn't know ?

      a. that she's a lucky girl

      b. that her boyfriend is cheating on her

      c. that love can come again

****

15. In *Come On Let's Go,* what does Ritchie Valens want you to tell him ?

      a. that it's time to go upstairs

      b. that it's not time to say goodbye

      c. that you'll never leave him

16. Although she loves *My Boy Lollipop*, what doesn't Millie Small want to do ?

       a. share him with her so-called friends

       b. let him know how she feels

       c. overdose on his sweetness

****

17. In *Maybe*, what did the Chantels pray for the Lord to send you ?

       a. their love

       b. a rose and a Baby Ruth

       c. a way back into their heart

****

18. In *Rag Doll,* if they could, what would the Four Seasons change her sad rags into ?

       a. satin and lace

       b. glad rags

       c. sable and mink

****

19. What specifically does Bobby Vee not want you to ask when he says *Please Don't Ask About Barbara* ?

       a. if she's found somebody new

       b. if that's her real name

       c. who she's going out with now

****

20. What did Sheb Wooley's *Purple People Eater* really want to do ?

       a. be accepted for who he is

       b. eat purple people

       c. get a job in a rock & roll band

HARDER QUESTIONS: Worth 2 points each — 4 points if you can answer the question without the three choices !

****

1. According to Mary Wells in *The One Who Really Loves You,* why does Jennie want you ?
   a. because she thinks she has to have everyone
   b. because she's crazy
   c. because she wants to make all the other girls jealous

****

2. In *Norman,* when Jimmy called her, where was Sue Thompson ?
   a. in the living room watching television with Norman
   b. parked all alone with Norman
   c. in the pool swimming with Norman

****

3. What do the Bachelors what their *Diane* to do for them ?
   a. say the word
   b. smile
   c. dance

****

4. In *Could This Be Magic,* if it is, then what do the Dubs say that magic really is ?
   a. love
   b. a crazy scene
   c. unreal

****

5. In *Gee Whiz,* what happens to Bob & Earl when you kiss them ?
   a. they feel all funny inside
   b. they go on a roller coaster ride
   c. they thrill

ANSWERS

****

1. a. hold their hand
2. b. the chance to have you near
3. a. cold as ice
4. b. when the whippoorwill calls
5. c. Waterloo
6. b. a grizzly bear
7. c. his baby's lips
8. a. you walked away
9. b. treat her like you did before
10. c. you
11. b. hanging from an oak tree
12. c. twenty-four
13. a. because you belong to him
14. a. that she's a lucky girl
15. c. that you'll never leave him
16. b. let him know how she feels
17. a. their love
18. b. glad rags
19. a. if she's found somebody new
20. c. get a job in a rock & roll band

****

HARDER QUESTIONS--Answers

1. a. because she thinks she has to have everyone
2. b. parked all alone with Norman
3. b. smile
4. a. love
5. c. they thrill

1. According to Elvis Presley in *Jailhouse Rock,* who was the rhythm section ?
>   a. the Jordanaires
>   b. the Purple Gang
>   c. the crew from Death Row

****

2. What does Johnny Mathis admit *It's Not For Me to Say* about you ?
>   a.   that you'll always care
>   b. how long he'll love you
>   c. whether you can see other guys

****

3. *Under the Boardwalk* the Drifters can hear the happy sounds of a _____.
>   a. little baby
>   b. carousel
>   c. clown

****

4. In *Shout! Shout! (Knock Yourself Out)*, what does Ernie Maresca want to do to liven up the scene ?
>   a. bring out the booze
>   b. turn the lights down low
>   c. turn the jukebox up loud

****

5. The Marvelettes tell their *Playboy* acquaintance that he'd better find himself another _____.
>   a. bunny
>   b. toy
>   c. place to stay

6. In *Why Do Fools Fall in Love,* what do Frankie Lymon & the Teenagers say lovers await ?

    a. words of love

    b. the break of day

    c. a smile from your lips

****

7. In *Can't Get Used to Losing You,* what does Andy Williams say he's going to live his whole life doing ?

    a. loving you

    b. forgetting you

    c. looking for you

****

8. Because *I Walk the Line,* how does Johnny Cash find himself when each day is through ?

    a. on pins and needles

    b. bored

    c. alone

****

9. What did Elvis Presley use to do to the *Little Sister* ?

    a. pull her pigtails and pinch her nose

    b. tell her dirty jokes

    c. make her cry

****

10. What do the Hollywood Argyles say *Alley-Oop* is the king of ?

    a. the mountain men

    b. the dinosaurs

    c. the jungle jive

11. If he were a *Tower of Strength,* what would Gene McDaniels do ?

     a. he'd tell you that he doesn't need you

     b. he'd beg you to stay

     c. he'd remove all your fears

****

12. For how long will Connie Francis be on *Vacation* ?

     a. for the rest of her life

     b. as long as there's love in the air

     c. until the start of the fall

****

13. Now that they have discovered they've become *Cathy's Clown,* what things don't the Everly Brothers want from her anymore ?

     a. her excuses

     b. her kisses

     c. her mindless gossip

****

14. In *Fools Rush In,* how did Rick Nelson feel when he first met you ?

     a. like his life had just begun

     b. nervous and scared

     c. as though he were about to ride a roller coaster

****

15. How long does Sam Cooke say they're going to stay and have their *Good Times* ?

     a. for the whole night through

     b. until the stars don't shine

     c. until they soothe their soul

16. What has happened to Lesley Gore that has her say that now it's *Judy's Turn to Cry*?
     a. she's cried her last tear
     b. she won't let Judy play on her basketball team
     c. Johnny's come back to her

****

17. In *Drip Drop,* when his friend gave him the news that Dion's girlfriend had given him the slip, what did Dion reply?
     a. thanks for the tip
     b. mind your own business and shut your lip
     c. it's the drugs that put her on that trip

****

18. Why is it that the Drifters say *I'll Take You Home*?
     a. because you're their woman
     b. because they're lonely, too
     c. because there's nothing more to do

****

19. In *You've Really Got a Hold On Me,* the Miracles say that they don't like you but they _____.
     a. love you
     b. are stuck with you
     c. can put up with you

****

20. Though *He's Sure the Boy I Love,* the Crystals admit that he's not the boy _____.
     a. that they'd want to bring home to mom and dad
     b. who shows them love and affection
     c. they'd been dreaming of

HARDER QUESTIONS: Worth 2 points each — 4 points if you can answer the question without the three choices !

****

1. In *Wonderful! Wonderful!* where is Johnny Mathis standing with you, gazing at the earth and sky, when he turns to you and you melt into his arms ?
   - a. on their balcony
   - b. on the top of a hill
   - c. in paradise

****

2. According to Nino Tempo & April Stevens, when the *Deep Purple* falls, what happens ?
   - a. it's the start of the blues
   - b. the stars begin to twinkle in the night
   - c. love fills the air

****

3. What is it that the Skyliners say *This I Swear* ?
   - a. that they will never cheat on you again
   - b. that they won't ever swear again
   - c. that their lips will kiss nobody else

****

4. What does Dion call his *Little Diane* ?
   - a. a dream come true
   - b. a goddess in pigtails
   - c. a little evil child

****

5. According to the Orlons in *Don't Hang Up,* where were they when they unexpectedly bumped into their boyfriend ?
   - a. at the record hop
   - b. in the movie theater
   - c. in the shopping mall

ANSWERS

****

1. b. the Purple Gang
2. a. that you'll always care
3. b. carousel
4. c. turn the jukebox up loud
5. b. toy
6. b. the break of day
7. a. loving you
8. c. alone
9. a. pull her pigtails and pinch her nose
10. c. the jungle jive
11. a. he'd tell you that he doesn't need you
12. c. until the start of the fall
13. b. her kisses
14. a. like his life had just begun
15. c. until they soothe their soul
16. c. Johnny's come back to her
17. b. mind your own business and shut your lip
18. b. because they're lonely, too
19. a. love you
20. c. they'd been dreaming of

****

HARDER QUESTIONS--Answers

1. b. on the top of a hill
2. b. the stars begin to twinkle in the night
3. c. that their lips will kiss nobody else
4. c. a little evil child
5. a. at the record hop

1. After they go to the *Chapel of Love,* what do the Dixie Cups say they'll never be anymore ?

   a. free
   b. happy
   c. lonely

****

2. In *All Shook Up,* Elvis Presley calls his girl his

————————————.

   a. f laming star
   b. buttercup
   c. one desire

****

3. In *Big Girls Don't Cry,* what happened that showed the Four Seasons that big girls do cry ?

   a. you cried when they broke your Beatles albums
   b. your mama said you cried in bed
   c. they saw you cry tears of joy

****

4. In *It Hurts to Be In Love,* because Gene Pitney is in love with somebody who considers him as only a friend, what is the only way he can keep her ?

   a. by chaining her to his bed
   b. by dreaming
   c. by keeping it to himself

****

5. What does Lorne Greene say that people can't explain about the grave that contains *Ringo* ?

   a. why no flowers can grow above the grave
   b. why there's a tarnished star above the name
   c. why there are so many beetles there

6. What is Dee Dee Sharp going to *Ride* ?
      a. her pony
      b. the roller coaster
      c. a wave of love

****

7. In *There! I've Said It Again*, Bobby Vinton says he's
   loved you since when ?
      a. since you were nine or ten
      b. since heaven knows when
      c. since he first opened his eyes to love again

****

8. Frankie Avalon suggests to *Just Ask Your Heart* for
   the answer to what question ?
      a. Who loves only you?
      b. Where is love?
      c. Are you too young to fall in love?

****

9. Because he's *Close to Cathy*, what is it that Mike
   Clifford knows?
      a. that she's not the girl she pretends to be
      b. where she is—twenty-four hours a day
      c. what she's dreaming of

****

10. According to Barbara Lynn, *You'll Lose a Good
    Thing* if you should do what ?
      a. lose her
      b. drop out of school
      c. cheat on a friend

11. What does Pat Boone ask *Speedy Gonzales* to do ?
   a. slow down
   b. come home
   c. kick the habit

****

12. For how long will Johnny Burnette be *Dreamin'* ?
   a. for the rest of his life
   b. until his dreamin' comes true
   c. until you're in his arms once again

****

13. What do Kathy Young & the Innocents say *A Thousand Stars* in the sky are like ?
   a. the stars in your eyes
   b. the sunshine of your smile
   c. grains of sand in the sea of love

****

14. Under what condition does Bobby Vee say you should *Run to Him* ?
   a. if walking is too slow
   b. if you're through running around
   c. if you've found another guy who satisfies you more than he does

****

15. Where is Lee Dorsey sitting, waiting for his *Ya Ya* ?
   a. in La La
   b. outside the supermarket
   c. at the entrance to the coal mine

16. What does Gene McDaniels say that *Chip Chip* is chipping away at ?
>   a. your wall of indifference
>   b. your tower of strength
>   c. your mansion of love

****

17. In *Everybody Loves a Lover,* who do the Shirelles say is the most popular personality ?
>   a. they are
>   b. their boyfriend is
>   c. lovers in love are

****

18. What did *Donna the Prima Donna* do to Dion ?
>   a. she made love to him
>   b. she broke his heart
>   c. she sent him packing

****

19. Because *She's Not You,* what does Elvis Presley have to be careful not to do when he dances with her?
>   a. step on her feet
>   b. start crying
>   c. whisper your name

****

20. Who do *Those Oldies But Goodies* remind Little Caesar & the Romans of ?
>   a. you
>   b. the person they used to be
>   c. the places they used to go

HARDER QUESTIONS: Worth 2 points each — 4 points if you can answer the question without the three choices !

****

1. In *Kiss Me Sailor,* what does Diane Renay like to do with her sailor boy during his shore leave ?
   - a. go dancing and romancing
   - b. snuggle up and watch the late late show
   - c. any old thing that he wants to do

****

2. In *Sally, Go 'Round the Roses,* what do the Jaynetts say is the saddest thing ?
   - a. to be forgotten and forsaken
   - b. to run away from home
   - c. to see your baby with another girl

****

3. According to Curtis Lee, what is the *Little Girl* wearing ?
   - a. a pony-tail and high-topped sneakers
   - b. a groovy mini-skirt
   - c. black silk stockings

****

4. According to the Olympics, who is it that does the *Hully Gully* ?
   - a. everybody who's not square
   - b. mama, papa and baby
   - c. everyone around the world

****

5. According to Johnny Preston, what was the name of the lovely Indian maid who loved *Running Bear* ?
   - a. Little White Dove
   - b. Walking Tree
   - c. Pretty Gypsy Eyes

ANSWERS

****

1. c. lonely
2. b. buttercup
3. b. your mama said you cried in bed
4. c. by keeping it to himself
5. b. why there's a tarnished star above the name
6. a. her pony
7. b. since heaven knows when
8. a. Who loves only you?
9. c. what she's dreaming of
10. a. lose her
11. b. come home
12. b. until his dreamin' comes true
13. a. the stars in your eyes
14. c. if you've found another guy who satisfies you more than he does
15. a. in La La
16. c. your mansion of love
17. a. they are
18. b. she broke his heart
19. c. whisper your name
20. a. you

****

HARDER QUESTIONS--Answers

1. b. snuggle up and watch the late late show
2. c. to see your baby with another girl
3. c. black silk stockings
4. b. mama, papa and baby
5. a. Little White Dove

1. If you *Dance With Me,* what do the Drifters say might happen when the music ends?

      a. you and they will be lovers
      b. you'll ask them to dance with you again
      c. the evening might end, too

****

2. Because he found the place for *Lovers Who Wander,* what does Dion now call himself?

      a. the loneliest person in the world
      b. the luckiest guy in the human race
      c. a three-time loser

****

3. In *What Is Love,* what do the Playmates say she shows you when she talks?

      a. her teeth
      b. her ignorance
      c. a dimple

****

4. Because the Shangri-Las say *I Can Never Go Home Anymore,* what word describes their situation?

      a. sad
      b. bummer
      c. free

****

5. In *Ready Teddy,* what is Little Richard ready to do?

      a. make love to you
      b. go home with you
      c. rock & roll

6. Because *There's a Moon Out Tonight,* what do the Capris want to do ?
- a. go dancing all night long
- b. go strolling through the park
- c. make romance

****

7. What do the Highwaymen say that *Michael* will do ?
- a. row the boat ashore
- b. trim the sails
- c. drown in the sea of love

****

8. What is it that the Sensations hear that makes them ask you to *Let Me In* ?
- a. loud noises
- b. music
- c. another woman

****

9. In *You Don't Know What You've Got (Until You Lose It),* what does Ral Donner say he did with all the love you gave him ?
- a. he sold it to the junk man
- b. he sealed it in a letter and mailed it to himself
- c. he misused it

****

10. To be *Slow Twistin',* Chubby Checker says you don't need speed but a lot of _____.
- a. nerve
- b. soul
- c. skill

11. Because she was *Only Sixteen,* what does Sam Cooke say she was too young to do ?

      a. raise a family

      b. handle the stress

      c.   fall in love

****

12. When you *Do the Bird,* what does Dee Dee Sharp want you to do with her ?

      a. chirp

      b. wave your hands and reach up high

      c. take her to the sky above

****

13. In *He Will Break Your Heart,* what does Jerry Butler say the other boy is trying to do to you and him ?

      a. tear you two apart

      b. end your romance before it even starts

      c. begin a new love that will reach the stars

****

14. Though *You're a Thousand Miles Away,* what do the Heartbeats say will happen soon ?

      a. a phone call will bring you both close together again

      b. they'll be home

      c. you'll discover that distance cannot destroy true love

****

15. What does Linda Scott tell you to *Don't Bet Money Honey* regarding ?

      a. that the stock market will keep going up

      b. that love is a sure thing

      c. that your love and hers will last

16. Even though his girlfriend treats him like a
    Rubber Ball, what doesn't Bobby Vee do ?
    - a. put her down
    - b. want to play ball
    - c. let himself be bounced around

****

17. Although the Coasters say *Poison Ivy* is pretty
    as a daisy, they also caution you that she's

    _____.
    - a. crazy
    - b. lazy
    - c. nasty

****

18. Even though it is crowded, what is there still room
    for in Elvis Presley's *Heartbreak Hotel* ?
    - a. poets and dreamers
    - b. lonely musicians
    - c. broken-hearted lovers

****

19. According to Tommy Edwards, what must happen,
    because It's *All In the Game* ?
    - a. someone must win, someone must lose
    - b. many a tear has to fall
    - c. the game must end sometime

****

20. What do the Rockyfellers say that *Killer Joe*
    should do ?
    - a. dance with only them
    - b. get a job
    - c. stay out of their way

HARDER QUESTIONS: Worth 2 points each — 4 points if you can answer the question without the three choices !

****

1. According to Chubby Checker, how do you do the *Popeye* dance ?
   - a. you clap your hands and thumb your thumbs
   - b. you flex your arms and take a stance
   - c. you turn around as if in a trance

****

2. According to the Browns, what would *The Old Lamplighter* do wherever he would go ?
   - a. he'd tell stories of the past
   - b. he'd bring a little love to the day
   - c. he'd make the night a little brighter

****

3. In *What Kind of Love Is This?* what do Joey Dee & the Starliters say that love is making them act like ?
   - a. a teenage Romeo
   - b. a psycho case
   - c. a daydreaming fool

****

4. In Johnny Otis' *Willie & the Hand Jive,* what did Willie do while performing the dance that was really a treat for the family ?
   - a. he spun around at the same time
   - b. he did the Hand Jive with his feet
   - c. he danced with baby Sis

****

5. According to Jimmy Dean, how many people did *Big Bad John* save from the cave-in at the mine ?
   - a. 20
   - b. 75
   - c. 200

ANSWERS

****

1. a. you and they will be lovers
2. b. the luckiest guy in the human race
3. c. a dimple
4. a. sad
5. c. rock & roll
6. b. go strolling through the park
7. a. row the boat ashore
8. b. music
9. c. he misused it
10. b. soul
11. c. fall in love
12. c. take her to the sky above
13. a. tear you two apart
14. b. they'll be home
15. c. that your love and hers will last
16. a. put her down
17. a. crazy
18. c. broken-hearted lovers
19. b. many a tear has to fall
20. a. dance with only them

****

HARDER QUESTIONS--Answers

1. a. you clap your hands and strum your thumb
2. c. he'd make the night a little brighter
3. b. a psycho case
4. b. he did the Hand Jive with his feet
5. a. 20

1. When other people say *He's a Rebel,* where will the Crystals be ?
   a. hiding behind him
   b. standing by his side
   c. at home, calling his lawyer

****

2. Although *She Can't Find Her Keys,* what does Paul Petersen say she can find with ease ?
   a. an autograph of Fabian
   b. her homework
   c. an excuse to go home

****

3. How long do the Drifters say *This Magic Moment* will last ?
   a. for a long time
   b. until the next kiss
   c. forever, until the end of time

****

4. In *Who's Sorry Now,* what did Connie Francis try to do ?
   a. leave you
   b. frighten you
   c. warn you

****

5. Although Guy Mitchell has *Heartaches By the Number,* what does he say will happen the day he stops counting ?
   a. his world will end
   b. a new life will begin
   c. he'll be ready for algebra

6. What do the Ad Libs' *Boy From New York City* have that is the finest in town ?

    a. a penthouse
    b. a Lamborghini
    c. a rock & roll band

****

7. Although the Four Seasons say that they could love you, what is it that stops them and instead makes them say *Bye, Bye, Baby (Baby Goodbye)*?

    a. there's a wedding band on their finger
    b. they're not ready for a long–term commitment
    c. they really don't like you

****

8. What does Gary U.S. Bonds plan to do until *Quarter to Three* ?

    a. drink his blues away
    b. dance
    c. wait impatiently for school to end

****

9. The Young Lions say that *Maybe Someday* you will see that _____.

    a. you were wrong
    b. you were meant for them
    c. not every problem has a simple solution

****

10. In *Everyday,* what does Buddy Holly ask whether you long for ?

    a. true love from him
    b. fame and fortune
    c. a better life

11. What does Roy Orbison say he'll never do to his
    Blue Angel ?

> a. question why she's always blue
> b. say goodbye
> c. call her a devil

****

12. In *Tonight's the Night,* what are the Shirelles
    afraid might happen from wanting you so much ?

> a. they may find their dreams torn apart
> b. they may drive you away from them
> c. they may do something they'll regret later on

****

13. What does Carl Perkins have in his *Matchbox*?

> a. old matches
> b. faded photographs
> c. his clothes

****

14. While they're *Having a Party,* what is Sam Cooke
    and his friends listening to as they are dancing to
    the music ?

> a. a rockin' band
> b. the radio
> c. the sound of cars passing by
>   in the night

****

15. According to Bobby Vinton in *Mr. Lonely*, why is
    he so far away from home ?

> a. because he's a soldier
> b. because he's a wanderer
> c. because he drives a truck

16. In *Sink the Bismarck,* what does Johnny Horton say made the ship so special ?
    a. it could hold more sailors than any other ship
    b. it was built in less time than any before it
    c. it was the fastest ship that ever sailed the sea

17. In *Wake Up Little Susie,* why are the Everly Brothers and their date going to be getting home so late ?
    a. Susie fell asleep in the back seat
    b. their car ran out of gas
    c. they fell asleep at the movies

18. Why will Connie Francis *Follow the Boys* ?
    a. because she knows she'll find her own true love along the way
    b. because she's tired of following the girls
    c. because life is more exciting that way

19. Terry Stafford has *Suspicion* that when you tell him you want to see him tomorrow, he can't help but think that you're _____.
    a. going to secretly see him tonight
    b. meeting someone else tonight
    c. planning a surprise party for him

20. In *Don't Play That Song,* how old was the girlfriend who walked out on Ben E. King ?
    a. twenty-one
    b. fourteen
    c. seventeen

HARDER QUESTIONS: Worth 2 points each — 4 points if you can answer the question without the three choices!

****

1. Where did the Shangri-Las meet the *Leader of the Pack*?

       a. at the drive-in
       b. at the cemetary
       c. at the candy store

****

2. From what state is Chuck Berry's *Johnny B. Goode*?

       a. Louisiana
       b. Mississippi
       c. Tennessee

****

3. What kind of establishment is the wooden building Jimmy Gilmer & the Fireballs nicknamed the *Sugar Shack*?

       a. a bar
       b. a coffeehouse
       c. a bowling alley

****

4. According to Mark Dinning, what did the *Teen Angel* return to the stalled automobile on the railroad tracks to retrieve?

       a. her sweater
       b. her boyfriend's high school ring
       c. the car keys

****

5. In *I Need Your Love Tonight,* what does Elvis Presley have on high?

       a. his lovin'
       b. his hopes
       c. his hi-fi

ANSWERS

****

1. b. standing by his side
2. a. an autograph of Fabian
3. c. forever, until the end of time
4. c. warn you
5. a. his world will end
6. a. a penthouse
7. a. there's a wedding band on their finger
8. b. dance
9. b. you were meant for them
10. a. true love from him
11. b. say goodbye
12. a. they may find their dreams torn apart
13. c. his clothes
14. b. the radio
15. a. because he's a soldier
16. c. it was the fastest ship that ever sailed the sea
17. c. they fell asleep at the movies
18. a. because she knows she'll find her own true love
    along the way
19. b. meeting someone else tonight
20. c. seventeen

****

HARDER QUESTIONS--Answers

1. c. at the candy store
2. a. Louisiana
3. b. a coffeehouse
4. b. her boyfriend's high school ring
5. c. his hi-fi

1. According to Buddy Holly & the Crickets in *That'll Be the Day*, the day his baby says that she's going to leave will be the day _____.
>   a. he knows she loves him
>   b. he says he's sorry
>   c. he dies

****

2. In *Beep Beep*, what model car is trying to pass the Playmates' Cadillac ?
>   a. a Rabbit
>   b. a Rambler
>   c. a Pinto

****

3. In *Chantilly Lace*, what time does The Big Bopper's date want him to come by ?
>   a. six o'clock
>   b. eight o'clock
>   c. as soon as possible

****

4. In *Big Man in Town*, what do the Four Seasons say your folks will one day do ?
>   a. apologize to them
>   b. welcome them
>   c. stop bugging them

****

5. In *I Can't Stop Loving You*, what does Ray Charles say he's resigned himself to doing ?
>   a. living in memories of the lonesome times
>   b. dreaming of a love that he will never know
>   c. wandering the streets and back-alleys looking for love

6. What happens when *Ruby Baby* looks at Dion ?

        a. she starts giggling

        b. he gets all nervous deep inside

        c. she sets his soul aflame

****

7. How does Paul Petersen feel when he walks alongside *My Dad* ?

        a. like a fish out of water

        b. ten feet tall

        c. like a little kid

****

8. In *Another Saturday Night,* what does Sam Cooke say he'd be doing if he were home ?

        a. waiting for your phone call

        b. watching *Leave It To Beaver*

        c. swinging with two chicks

****

9. By what time is Lee Dorsey already up and *Working In the Coal Mine* ?

        a. five o'clock in the morning

        b. before dawn

        c. midnight

****

10. Although the Drifters say it's okay to dance with others in *Save the Last Dance For Me,* what do they remind you about after the evening is through ?

        a. that they've been paying for all the drinks

        b. that you've got the car keys

        c. that you shouldn't forget who's taking you home

11. To what query does Johnny Mathis refer when he replies *The Twelfth of Never*?
   a. until how long he'll wait for you to return
   b. how long he'll love you until
   c. what day precedes the thirteenth of Never

****

12. What is Gene McDaniels, in *A Hundred Pounds of Clay*, going to thank the Lord every night for?
   a. the birds in the sky
   b. his profession in clay-modeling
   c. the arms that are holding him tight

****

13. According to Betty Everett in *Shoop Shoop Song (It's In His Kiss)*, what does his kiss tell you?
   a. what's on his mind
   b. if he loves you
   c. if he gargled earlier

****

14. In *Goin' Out of My Head*, why do Little Anthony & the Imperials feel an unrequited love each morning they see their lady-hopeful?
   a. because she's already married
   b. because they're too shy to say hello
   c. because she just walks past them

****

15. What do the Penguins hope and pray in *Earth Angel*?
   a. that one day they'll marry you and take you home
   b. that they'll be the vision of your happiness
   c. that you'll come and visit them in their dreams

16. Besides saying *I Want to Walk You Home,* what else does Fats Domino ask if he can do ?

    a. hold your hand

    b. see you tomorrow

    c. call you up

****

17. What place is waiting *26 Miles* across the sea for the Four Preps ?

    a. Santa Catalina

    b. Hawaii

    c. paradise

****

18. In *(Let Me Be Your) Teddy Bear,* why doesn't Elvis Presley want to be a lion ?

    a. because they aren't loved enough

    b. because they get hungry too easily

    c. because they play too rough

****

19. According to Don Gibson in *Oh, Lonesome Me,* what is everybody going out and doing ?

    a. dancing

    b. getting stoned

    c. having fun

****

20. In *New Orleans,* what does Gary U.S. Bonds say is blooming on the vine ?

    a. the honeysuckle

    b. oleander

    c. a daisy

HARDER QUESTIONS: Worth 2 points each — 4 points if you can answer the question without the three choices !

****

1. In *Volare*, what does Bobby Rydell want to leave behind ?

      a. all the confusion and disillusion

      b. all his worries and his fears

      c. all the daily hangups and hassles

****

2. Although people call it a *Teen-Age Crush*, what does Tommy Sands say they can't believe ?

      a. that it could ever last

      b. that it can be taken seriously

      c. that it's real

****

3. In *Midnight Mary*, where does Joey Powers want to meet Mary ?

      a. behind the malt-shop

      b. at the same place they always go

      c. underneath the bleachers

****

4. What do the Chimes ask if you ever tried to do *Once In a While* ?

      a. fall in love

      b. walk a thin line

      c. give one little thought to them

****

5. In *Greenback Dollar,* the Kingston Trio say that some people say they're a no-count while others say that they are _____.

      a. no good

      b. misunderstood

      c. greedy

ANSWERS

****

1. c. he dies
2. b. a Rambler
3. b. eight o'clock
4. b. welcome them
5. a. living in memories of the lonesome times
6. c. she sets his soul aflame
7. b. ten feet tall
8. c. swinging with two chicks
9. a. five o'clock in the morning
10. c. that you shouldn't forget who's taking you home
11. b. how long he'll love you until
12. c. the arms that are holding him tight
13. b. if he loves you
14. c. because she just walks past them
15. b. that they'll be the vision of your happiness
16. a. hold your hand
17. a. Santa Catalina
18. a. because they aren't loved enough
19. c. having fun
20. a. the honeysuckle

****

HARDER QUESTIONS--Answers

1. a. all the confusion and disillusion
2. c. that it's real
3. b. at the same place they always go
4. c. give one little thought to them
5. a. no good

1. In *My Boyfriend's Back,* what will the Angels' boyfriend restore ?

       a. a lasting love

       b. their peace of mind

       c. their reputation

****

2. What does the *Stranger in Town* do to Del Shannon?

       a. he follows him to every town

       b. he spreads false rumors about him

       c. he tries to steal his girl

****

3. In *Maybe Baby,* what do Buddy Holly & the Crickets feel they'll have one day ?

       a. true love

       b. you

       c. a successful rock & roll career

****

4. What does Chuck Berry tell *Carol* that he's going to learn to do if it takes him all night and day ?

       a. love her

       b. dance

       c. read

****

5. In *Everybody's Somebody's Fool,* Connie Francis knows that, even though she'll be hurt by her boyfriend whenever she sees him, what does she concede ?

       a. that one day, she'll forget all about him

       b. that love will eventually bring them together

       c. that she'll come running back for more

6. In *Boys,* what have the Shirelles been told happens when a boy kisses a girl ?

    a. he takes a trip around the world

    b. he's in love to stay

    c. a star falls from the sky

****

7. What is it that you do after you say you love them that makes the Fleetwoods call themselves *Mr. Blue* ?

    a. you go out on the sly

    b. you squeeze them so tightly

    c. you say things that make them feel like the heavens above

****

8. In *Don't Be Cruel,* where can you find Elvis Presley ?

    a. in the school lunchroom

    b. in jail

    c. sitting all alone

****

9. In *Tutti-Frutti,* what is the name of Little Richard's girlfriend who drives him crazy ?

    a. Mazie

    b. Daisy

    c. Anastasie

****

10. According to Frankie Avalon, when a girl changes from *Bobby Sox to Stockings,* what does she begin trading her baby toys for ?

    a. trophies

    b. diamonds

    c. boys

11. What does Ben E. King see growing in *Spanish Harlem* ?

      a. a red rose

      b. poverty and despair

      c. a new generation

****

12. In *Cool Jerk,* when others look at the Capitols as if they're fools, they know that deep inside the people know they're _____.

      a. just foolin' around

      b. hip

      c. cool

****

13. Who did Bobby Day's *Rockin' Robin* go steady with ?

      a. the buzzard

      b. a raven

      c. another robin

****

14. In *Hey! Baby,* what does Bruce Channel want to know ?

      a. what your name is

      b. if you'll be his girl

      c. if you'll come dancing
         with him tonight

****

15. If Del Shannon and his girlfriend have to *Keep Searchin',* what will they follow to guide them ?

      a. the sun

      b. their dreams

      c. the yellow-brick road

16. While *Walkin' In the Rain,* how do the Ronettes envision the boy they may one day meet ?
   a. he'll be shy and good-looking
   b. he'll be the envy of all the other girls
   c. he'll be their dream-baby

****

17. As *The Great Pretender,* what is it that the Platters are pretending ?
   a. that they're great
   b. that one day you'll be their queen
   c. that you're still around

****

18. Because *You Send Me,* what is it that Sam Cooke says he's finding himself wanting to do ?
   a. marry you and take you home
   b. send you somewhere you've never been before
   c. ask you out on a date

****

19. Why does Steve Lawrence say that there could never be a *Portrait of My Love* ?
   a. because there ain't nothing like the real thing
   b. because nobody could ever paint a dream
   c. because no one knows the true color of his love

****

20. According to Miss Toni Fisher, why is it that now *The Big Hurt* begins ?
   a. because now you're gone
   b. because the memory of the good times has faded away
   c. because all the little lies have finally caught up with her

HARDER QUESTIONS: Worth 2 points each — 4 points if you can answer the question without the three choices !
****

1. According to Elvis Presley, how does *King Creole* hold his guitar ?

      a. by his side
      b. like it's his baby
      c. like a Tommy-gun
****

2. In *Goodbye Baby,* what does Jack Scott add ?

  a. that you were wrong
  b. that you know where to find him
  c. that there's nothing good about saying goodbye
****

3. According to Buddy Holly, when is it that *Peggy Sue Got Married* ?

      a. last night
      b. not long ago
      c. a month ago
****

4. In *When,* what is it that the Kalin Twins want to know ?

     a. when does summer school begin
     b. when is it too young to be in love
     c. when will you be theirs
****

5. What are the names of the two guys the Marvelettes recommend selecting from so that you *Don't Mess With Bill* ?

      a. Tommy and Bobby
      b. Frank and Jim
      c. Ringo and Phil

ANSWERS

****

1. c. their reputation
2. a. he follows him to every town
3. b. you
4. b. dance
5. c. that she'll come running back for more
6. a. he takes a trip around the world
7. a. you go out on the sly
8. c. sitting all alone
9. b. Daisy
10. c. boys
11. a. a red rose
12. c. cool
13. b. a raven
14. b. if you'll be his girl
15. a. the sun
16. a. he'll be shy and good-looking
17. c. that you're still around
18. a. marry you and take you home
19. b. because nobody could ever paint a dream
20. a. because now you're gone

****

HARDER QUESTIONS--Answers

1. c. like a Tommy-gun
2. a. that you were wrong
3. b. not long ago
4. c. when will you be theirs
5. b. Frank and Jim

ROCK

TITLES

QUESTIONS

If you're brave enough to test your skills,
here's a simple SCORING CHART:

(questions are worth 1 point each — "Harder Questions" are worth 2 points each . . . If you are able to identify the song without referring to the three choices, you receive twice the point value!)

If you score . . .

25+ Points: You probably STILL think it's 1957!
(Check your wardrobe!)

20–24: You probably paid more attention to
rock & roll than books & school!
(Check your report card!)

15–19: There's a lot of rock & roll memories
in your blood!
*(But maybe it's time to buy
a few more rock & roll LPs!)*

10–14: Don't you wish you'd listened more closely
to rock & roll?!
(It's never too late to be hip!)

0–9: Where were YOU when rock began to rule?!
*(Time to get experienced —
run to your music store now!!!)*

(note: all answers are derived from lyrics within the song)

1. They *holler and whistle,* they *Pony and Twist,* and
they rock *with Daddy G.*
   a. The Wah-Watusi/Orlons
   b. Let's Twist Again/Chubby Checker
   c. Bristol Stomp/Dovells

****

2. He wants her to love him before he *grows too old.*
   a. Donna/Ritchie Valens
   b. Dizzy Miss Lizzy/Larry Williams
   c. My Special Angel/Bobby Helms

****

3. When you *flashed those big brown eyes* his way,
he knew he *wanted you forevermore.*
   a. Hello Mary Lou/Ricky Nelson
   b. Little Devil/Neil Sedaka
   c. Oh, Pretty Woman/Roy Orbison

****

4. *All who love are blind.*
   a. Who's Sorry Now/Connie Francis
   b. Smoke Gets In Your Eyes/Platters
   c. I'm Sorry/Brenda Lee

****

5. When they get the newspaper, they *read it
through and through.*
   a. When/Kalin Twins
   b. Searchin'/Coasters
   c. Get a Job/Silhouettes

6. He says that *when you're rockin' and rollin',* you *can't hear your mama call.*
   a. Be-Bop Baby/Ricky Nelson
   b. Good Golly Miss Molly/Little Richard
   c. Rockin' Robin/Bobby Day

****

7. He advises you that *if she's the one, don't let her run away.*
   a. Catch a Falling Star/Perry Como
   b. All the Way/Frank Sinatra
   c. April Love/Pat Boone

****

8. *Little cable cars climb halfway to the stars.*
   a. Little Boxes/Pete Seger
   b. I Left My Heart In San Francisco/Tony Bennett
   c. Return to Me/Dean Martin

****

9. They *don't have happiness* and they guess they *never will ever again.*
   a. There Goes My Baby/Drifters
   b. Since I Don't Have You/Skyliners
   c. Big Man/Four Preps

****

10. That girl he sat beside *was awful cute* — and when they stopped, *she was holding hands* with him and his heart *was flying.*
    a. Volare/Bobby Rydell
    b. Palisades Park/Freddy Cannon
    c. Poetry In Motion/Johnny Tillotson

11. If the band slows down, they'll *yell for more.*
   a. Rock Around the Clock/Bill Haley & His Comets
   b. Be-Bop-A-Lula/Gene Vincent & His Blue Caps
   c. At The Hop/Danny & the Juniors

****

12. They say that you *put them down to size by telling dirty lies to* their *friends* — even their *father said to give her up.*
   a. Walk Like a Man/Four Seasons
   b. Stop and Think It Over/Dale & Grace
   c. Shop Around/Miracles

****

13. *Like a river flows surely to the sea,* so it goes that *some things are meant to be.*
   a. You Can Depend On Me/Brenda Lee
   b. Will You Love Me Tomorrow/Shirelles
   c. Can't Help Falling In Love/Elvis Presley

****

14. They *see you walk with another,* wishing it could be them, but they know *it can never be.*
   a. Mr. Blue/Fleetwoods
   b. To Know Him Is To Love Him/Teddy Bears
   c. Born Too Late/Poni-Tails

****

15. He found his *thrill* here.
   a. Blueberry Hill/Fats Domino
   b. Canadian Sunset/Andy Williams
   c. Just Walking In the Rain/Johnnie Ray

16. They ask whether there's *a letter in your bag for me.*
   a. Dedicated to the One I Love/Shirelles
   b. Take a Message to Mary/Everly Brothers
   c. Please Mr. Postman/Marvelettes

****

17. They *can't live without you;* they *love everything about you* — and they *can't help it if* they *feel this way.*
   a. Baby I Love You/Ronettes
   b. Do You Love Me/Contours
   c. You've Really Got a Hold On Me/Miracles

****

18. They ask the *Guardian Angels up above* to *take care of the one* they *love.*
   a. Little Star/Elegants
   b. Hushabye/Mystics
   c. Whispering Bells/Dell Vikings

****

19. *At the end of a river, the water stops its flow; at the end of a highway, there's no place you can go.*
   a. The End of the World/Skeeter Davis
   b. The End/Earl Grant
   c. No Particular Place to Go/Chuck Berry

****

20. Here *the chicks are kicks and the cats are cool.*
   a. Village of Love/Nathaniel Mayer
   b. Down By the Station/Four Preps
   c. Swingin' School/Bobby Rydell

HARDER QUESTIONS: Worth 2 points each — 4 points if you can NAME THAT TUNE without the three choices !

****

1. In the morning mist, *two lovers kissed and the world stood still.*

   a. Love Is a Many Splendored Thing/Four Aces
   b. Shangri-La/Four Coins
   c. Enchanted/Platters

****

2. He wants you to let him kiss your lips because *it's cold and your lips might freeze.*

   a. You Send Me/Sam Cooke
   b. Secretly/Jimmie Rodgers
   c. Don't Forbid Me/Pat Boone

****

3. When you said you were leaving tomorrow, he *said there'd be no sorrow* — that he'd *laugh when you walked away.*

   a. Goodbye Baby/Jack Scott
   b. A Little Bitty Tear/Burl Ives
   c. Oh Lonesome Me/Don Gibson

****

4. He wears a *polka-dot vest* and *a purple head band.*

   a. Pink Shoe Laces/Dodie Stevens
   b. Duke of Earl/Gene Chandler
   c. Tall Paul/Annette

****

5. You tell him you love him and say you'll be true, but then *you fly around with somebody new.*

   a. Butterfly/Andy Williams
   b. Glendora/Perry Como
   c. It's Not For Me to Say/Johnny Mathis

ANSWERS

****

1. c. Bristol Stomp/Dovells
2. b. Dizzy Miss Lizzy/Larry Williams
3. a. Hello Mary Lou/Ricky Nelson
4. b. Smoke Gets In Your Eyes/Platters
5. c. Get a Job/Silhouettes
6. b. Good Golly Miss Molly/Little Richard
7. c. April Love/Pat Boone
8. b. I Left My Heart In San Francisco/Tony Bennett
9. b. Since I Don't Have You/Skyliners
10. b. Palisades Park/Freddy Cannon
11. a. Rock Around the Clock/Bill Haley & His Comets
12. a. Walk Like a Man/Four Seasons
13. c. Can't Help Falling In Love/Elvis Presley
14. c. Born Too Late/Poni-Tails
15. a. Blueberry Hill/Fats Domino
16. c. Please Mr. Postman/Marvelettes
17. a. Baby I Love You/Ronettes
18. b. Hushabye/Mystics
19. b. The End/Earl Grant
20. c. Swingin' School/Bobby Rydell

****

HARDER QUESTIONS--Answers

1. a. Love Is a Many Splendored Thing/Four Aces
2. c. Don't Forbid Me/Pat Boone
3. b. A Little Bitty Tear/Burl Ives
4. a. Pink Shoe Laces/Dodie Stevens
5. a. Butterfly/Andy Williams

1. As he was *motivating over the hill,* he saw her *in a Coupe DeVille.*
   a. Start Movin' (In My Direction)/Sal Mineo
   b. Maybellene/Chuck Berry
   c. Party Doll/Buddy Knox

****

2. *Your daddy don't mind and your mommy don't mind* if they have another dance.
   a. Dance With Me/Drifters
   b. Let's Go, Let's Go, Let's Go/Hank Ballard & the Midnighters
   c. Stay/Maurice Williams & the Zodiacs

****

3. *Those devil eyes are bluer than the skies.*
   a. Baby Blue/Echoes
   b. Blue Velvet/Bobby Vinton
   c. Devil or Angel/Bobby Vee

****

4. Friends ask her if she's in love, and she always answers "yes" — *might as well confess if the answer is yes.*
   a. I've Told Every Little Star/Linda Scott
   b. Sweet Nothin's/Brenda Lee
   c. Let's Get Together/Hayley Mills

****

5. They are *only five years old;* their *baby is three.*
   a. Come Softly to Me/Fleetwoods
   b. Baby Talk/Jan & Dean
   c. I Want You to Be My Girl/Frankie Lymon & the Teenagers

6. They've got *some crazy little women there* and he's gonna get himself one.
   - a. Kansas City/Wilbert Harrison
   - b. Bimbombey/Jimmie Rodgers
   - c. Primrose Lane/Jerry Wallace

****

7. Their *eyes were wide open but all that* they *could see* was that the *chapel bells were calling for everyone but* them.
   - a. Our Day Will Come/Ruby & the Romantics
   - b. Mama Said/Shirelles
   - c. The Three Bells/Browns

****

8. He wonders whether *the answer lies in her kiss or in her eyes.*
   - a. Pretty Little Angel Eyes/Curtis Lee
   - b. It's All In the Game/Tommy Edwards
   - c. A Lover's Question/Clyde McPhatter

****

9. Can't you see *you're in* their *way* and that *you cramp* their *style.*
   - a. I've Had It/Bell Notes
   - b. Poison Ivy/Coasters
   - c. See You Later, Alligator/Bill Haley & His Comets

****

10. He is *but a fool* because you treat him cruel, but if you ever left him, he *would surely die.*
   - a. Oh! Carol/Neil Sedaka
   - b. Rubber Ball/Bobby Vee
   - c. Her Royal Majesty/James Darren

11. *If you don't behave,* he'll *walk right out on you.*
      a. Treat Me Nice/Elvis Presley
      b. Keep A Knockin'/Little Richard
      c. Tower of Strength/Gene McDaniels

****

12. He wants *a girl to call* his *own* — he hopes *she'll*
hear his pleas and *bring her love to him.*
      a. Venus/Frankie Avalon
      b. Diana/Paul Anka
      c. Dream Lover/Bobby Darin

****

13. He loves her with a love *so rare and true.*
      a. Peggy Sue/Buddy Holly
      b. April Love/Pat Boone
      c. Hula Love/Buddy Knox

****

14. *Oo-ee-oo-ah-ah-ting-tang-walla-walla-bing-*
bang.
      a. The Flying Saucer/Buchanan & Goodman
      b. Witch Doctor/David Seville
      c. Shimmy Shimmy Ko-Ko-Pop/Little Anthony
        & the Imperials

****

15. *Oh how happy now* they *can be making love*
underneath the apple tree.
      a. We Got Love/Bobby Rydell
      b. Denise/Randy & the Rainbows
      c. Bony Maronie/Larry Williams

16. They *smell smoke in the auditorium.*
        a. Smoke Gets In Your Eyes/Platters
        b. Charlie Brown/Coasters
        c. Trouble In Paradise/Crests

****

17. *You're not a kid anymore.*
        a. Mama Said/Shirelles
        b. Bobby's Girl/Marcie Blane
        c. Surrender/Elvis Presley

****

18. If they had left home at a quarter to nine, they'd *have had fun and plenty of time.*
        a. Wake Up Little Susie/Everly Brothers
        b. It's Late/Ricky Nelson
        c. Dum Dum/Brenda Lee

****

19. He's got *no time for geometry, arithmetic or history.*
        a. School Is Out/Gary U.S. Bonds
        b. Wonderful World/Sam Cooke
        c. Cindy's Birthday/Johnny Crawford

****

20. *"Don't put your faith in love, my boy,"* their *father said to* them.
        a. Walk Like a Man/Four Seasons
        b. Lemon Tree/Peter, Paul & Mary
        c. Zip-A-Dee-Doo-Dah/Bob B. Soxx & The Blue Jeans

HARDER QUESTIONS: Worth 2 points each — 4 points if you can NAME THAT TUNE without the three choices !

****

1. *The way they kiss, their happiness*—he wonders *will my aching heart ever mend.*

    a. I Wake Up Crying/Chuck Jackson
    b. The Girl of My Best Friend/Ral Donner
    c. Every Breath I Take/Gene Pitney

****

2. Although you *put the hurtin' on* him, It's a *natural fact* that he *likes it like that.*

    a. Baby Workout/Jackie Wilson
    b. I Like It Like That/Chris Kenner
    c. What'd I Say/Ray Charles

****

3. Sometimes they wonder why they *spend the lonely nights dreaming of you so*—the melody *haunts their reveries* as they are *once again with you* when love *was new and each kiss an inspiration.*

    a. Stardust/Billy Ward & His Dominoes
    b. Happy, Happy Birthday Baby/Tune Weavers
    c. Love Is Strange/Mickey & Sylvia

****

4. Somehow she *can't dismiss the memory of your kiss.*

    a. The Big Hurt/Miss Toni Fischer
    b. Sailor (Your Home Is the Sea)/Lolita
    c. My Heart Has a Mind of Its Own/Connie Francis

****

5. They're *made out of ticky-tacky* and *they all look just the same.*

    a. Paper Roses/Anita Bryant
    b. Little Boxes/Pete Seger
    c. I Left My Heart In San Francisco/Tony Bennett

ANSWERS

****

1. b. Maybellene/Chuck Berry
2. c. Stay/Maurice Williams & the Zodiacs
3. a. Baby Blue/Echoes
4. a. I've Told Every Little Star/Linda Scott
5. b. Baby Talk/Jan & Dean
6. a. Kansas City/Wilbert Harrison
7. b. Mama Said/Shirelles
8. c. A Lover's Question/Clyde McPhatter
9. c. See You Later, Alligator/Bill Haley & His Comets
10. a. Oh! Carol/Neil Sedaka
11. a. Treat Me Nice/Elvis Presley
12. c. Dream Lover/Bobby Darin
13. a. Peggy Sue/Buddy Holly
14. b. Witch Doctor/David Seville
15. c. Bony Maronie/Larry Williams
16. b. Charlie Brown/Coasters
17. b. Bobby's Girl/Marcie Blane
18. b. It's Late/Ricky Nelson
19. c. Cindy's Birthday/Johnny Crawford
20. b. Lemon Tree/Peter, Paul & Mary

****

HARDER QUESTIONS--Answers

1. b. The Girl of My Best Friend/Ral Donner
2. a. Baby Workout/Jackie Wilson
3. a. Stardust/Billy Ward & His Dominoes
4. c. My Heart Has a Mind of Its Own/Connie Francis
5. b. Little Boxes/Pete Seger

1. *You shake* his *nerves and you rattle* his *brain.*
   a. Lucille/Little Richard
   b. I'm In Love Again/Fats Domino
   c. Great Balls of Fire/Jerry Lee Lewis

   ****

2. *The jockey is the smoothest and the music is the coolest.*
   a. Mule Skinner Blues/Fendermen
   b. At The Hop/Danny & the Juniors
   c. Don't Knock the Rock/Bill Haley & His Comets

   ****

3. Although she *used to be a skinny little girl,* now she's *out of this world.*
   a. Venus In Blue Jeans/Jimmy Clanton
   b. Gina/Johnny Mathis
   c. Next Door to an Angel/Neil Sedaka

   ****

4. They only have to do this when they *want you in* their *arms* and when they *want you and all your charms.*
   a. Get a Job/Silhouettes
   b. Finger Poppin' Time/Hank Ballard & the Midnighters
   c. All I Have to Do Is Dream/Everly Brothers

   ****

5. They'll *go on living and keep on forgiving because you were* their *first love.*
   a. Ronnie/Four Seasons
   b. Mr. Lee/Bobbettes
   c. He's So Fine/Chiffons

6. They *remember that night in May when the stars were bright above.*
   - a. In The Still of the Night/Five Satins
   - b. There's a Moon Out Tonight/Capris
   - c. I Only Have Eyes For You/Flamingos

****

7. She *wishes that* she *knew if he knew* what she's dreaming of.
   - a. Goodbye Jimmy, Goodbye/Kathy Linden
   - b. Gidget/James Darren
   - c. Tammy/Debbie Reynolds

****

8. He doesn't want you to *take the train comin' down the track* and leave him *in misery.*
   - a. Without You/Johnny Tillotson
   - b. Lover Please/Clyde McPhatter
   - c. Corinna, Corinna/Ray Peterson

****

9. His baby said that *she was a bird.*
   - a. Rockin' Robin/Bobby Day
   - b. Bo Diddley/Bo Diddley
   - c. Turn Me Loose/Fabian

****

10. *She told* him *how she cared for* him *and that* they'd *never part, and so for the very first time,* he *gave away* his *heart.*
    - a. A Fool Such As I/Elvis Presley
    - b. Poor Little Fool/Ricky Nelson
    - c. Lonely Boy/Paul Anka

11. *It's a dance made for romance.*

    a. Bristol Stomp/Dovells

    b. The Wah-Watusi/Orlons

    c. Do the Surfer Stomp/Bruce Johnston

****

12. His love is *deeper than a wishing well* and *stronger than a magic spell.*

    a. Our Winter Love/Bill Pursell

    b. Mission Bell/Donnie Brooks

    c. I Can't Stop Loving You/Ray Charles

****

13. Each time they have a quarrel, *it almost breaks* their *heart* because they're afraid that *one day* they'll *have to part.*

    a. A Teenager In Love/Dion & the Belmonts

    b. He's Sure the Boy I Love/Crystals

    c. Don't Hang Up/Orlons

****

14. Her friends tell her to *go to him, run to him, say sweet-nothing things to him, and tell him he's the one.*

    a. Easier Said Than Done/Essex

    b. Sweet Nothin's/Brenda Lee

    c. Bobby's Girl/Marcie Blane

****

15. If she left them alone, they'd *have a happy home.*

    a. The Boll Weevil Song/Brook Benton

    b. Mother-In-Law/Ernie K-Doe

    c. If You Wanna Be Happy/Jimmy Soul

16. She *found out beyond a doubt* that *you were a playboy* who would go away and leave her blue.

      a. You Beat Me to the Punch/Mary Wells

      b. Playboy/Marvelettes

      c. Who's Sorry Now/Connie Francis

****

17. *Our dreams have magic because we'll always stay in love this way.*

      a. Our Day Will Come/Ruby & the Romantics

      b. So Much In Love/Tymes

      c. This Magic Moment/Drifters

****

18. *No such number; no such zone.*

      a. Shop Around/Miracles

      b. Return to Sender/Elvis Presley

      c. Busted/Ray Charles

****

19. It's so hard for them *to find a personality with charm like yours.*

      a. What's Your Name/Don & Juan

      b. Sweet Talkin' Guy/Chiffons

      c. Sherry/Four Seasons

****

20. Here *the world is sweet* and *at his feet.*

      a. Mexico/Bob Moore

      b. Al Di La/Emilio Pericoli

      c. Uptown/Crystals

HARDER QUESTIONS: Worth 2 points each — 4 points if you can NAME THAT TUNE without the three choices !

****

1. *Tomorrow is* their *special day.*
   - a. Chapel of Love/Dixie Cups
   - b. The Stripper/David Rose & His Orchestra
   - c. Young Lovers/Paul & Paula

****

2. *One thing you'll know for sure* is that she *won't be the one to fall in love with someone new — she'll love you* 'til she dies.
   - a. The Nitty Gritty/Shirley Ellis
   - b. I Can't Stay Mad at You/Skeeter Davis
   - c. I Know (You Don't Love Me No More)/Barbara George

****

3. When you leave them, their *golden rainbow disappears.*
   - a. Save It For Me/Four Seasons
   - b. Talking About My Baby/Impressions
   - c. You Don't Have to Be a Baby to Cry/Caravelles

****

4. *Oh what a mystery that seals so tight.*
   - a. You're the Reason I'm Living/Bobby Darin
   - b. I've Told Every Little Star/Linda Scott
   - c. Over the Mountain, Across the Sea/Johnnie & Joe

****

5. *Kiss by kiss and hand in hand, that's the way it all began.*
   - a. Step by Step/Crests
   - b. Book of Love/Monotones
   - c. To The Aisle/Five Satins

ANSWERS

****

1. c. Great Balls of Fire/Jerry Lee Lewis
2. b. At The Hop/Danny & the Juniors
3. c. Next Door to an Angel/Neil Sedaka
4. c. All I Have to Do Is Dream/Everly Brothers
5. a. Ronnie/Four Seasons
6. a. In The Still of the Night/Five Satins
7. c. Tammy/Debbie Reynolds
8. b. Lover Please/Clyde McPhatter
9. b. Bo Diddley/Bo Diddley
10. b. Poor Little Fool/Ricky Nelson
11. b. The Wah-Watusi/Orlons
12. b. Mission Bell/Donnie Brooks
13. a. A Teenager In Love/Dion & the Belmonts
14. a. Easier Said Than Done/Essex
15. b. Mother-In-Law/Ernie K-Doe
16. a. You Beat Me to the Punch/Mary Wells
17. a. Our Day Will Come/Ruby & the Romantics
18. b. Return to Sender/Elvis Presley
19. a. What's Your Name/Don & Juan
20. c. Uptown/Crystals

****

HARDER QUESTIONS--Answers

1. c. Young Lovers/Paul & Paula
2. b. I Can't Stay Mad at You/Skeeter Davis
3. c. You Don't Have to Be a Baby to Cry/Caravelles
4. c. Over the Mountain, Across the Sea/Johnnie & Joe
5. a. Step by Step/Crests

1. They want you to bring your love to them — *don't send it.*
   - a. A Thousand Miles Away/Heartbeats
   - b. Please Mr. Postman/Marvelettes
   - c. Walk Right Back/Everly Brothers

****

2. *Her tender lips are sweeter than honey.*
   - a. Dream Baby/Roy Orbison
   - b. Wolverton Mountain/Claude King
   - c. Roses Are Red/Bobby Vinton

****

3. After he got married, he suddenly became *the father of twins.*
   - a. Kisses Sweeter Than Wine/Jimmie Rodgers
   - b. Teen-Age Crush/Tommy Sands
   - c. Young Love/Sonny James

****

4. *You were all the world to* him — *all* his *dreams come true.*
   - a. Corinna, Corinna/Ray Peterson
   - b. Susie Darlin'/Robin Luke
   - c. Dreamin'/Johnny Burnette

****

5. *You didn't want him when he wanted you.*
   - a. Foolish Little Girl/Shirelles
   - b. Sally, Go 'Round the Roses/Jaynetts
   - c. Forget Him/Bobby Rydell

6. *Her name drives* him *insane.*

   a. Sheila/Tommy Roe

   b. Hello Mary Lou/Ricky Nelson

   c. Ya Ya/Lee Dorsey

****

7. They *look straight up at the ceiling above, thinking of the girl whom* they *will love — oh would it be soon when she exists.*

   a. When Will I Be Loved/Everly Brothers

   b. Image of a Girl/Safaris

   c. Where or When/Dion & the Belmonts

****

8. They wonder whether it could be the devil in them or whether *this is the way love's supposed to be.*

   a. I Wanna Love Him So Bad/Jelly Beans

   b. Goin' Out of My Head/Little Anthony & the Imperials

   c. Heat Wave/Martha & the Vandellas

****

9. *When you are near* her, her *heart skips a beat —* she *can hardly stand on* her *own two feet.*

   a. Angel Baby/Rosie & the Originals

   b. I Fall to Pieces/Patsy Cline

   c. I Love How You Love Me/Paris Sisters

****

10. He was *cruising and playing the radio.*

   a. Shout! Shout! (Knock Yourself Out)/Ernie Maresca

   b. No Particular Place to Go/Chuck Berry

   c. Love Came to Me/Dion

11. *Deep down inside he loves* her, *though he may run around.*
   a. Two Faces Have I/Lou Christie
   b. Maybe I Know/Lesley Gore
   c. He's a Rebel/Crystals

****

12. To do this dance, you've got to go *round and round, up and down,* then *one-two-three kick, one-to-three jump.*
   a. 1-2-3/Len Barry
   b. Do the Surfer Stomp/Bruce Johnston
   c. The Peppermint Twist/Joey Dee & the Starliters

****

13. *She's a teenage goddess from above, and she belongs to* him.
   a. Dream Lover/Bobby Darin
   b. Venus In Blue Jeans/Jimmy Clanton
   c. My Special Angel/Bobby Helms

****

14. It's the *dance of love.*
   a. Blame It On the Bossa Nova/Eydie Gorme
   b. The Fly/Chubby Checker
   c. The Loco-Motion/Little Eva

****

15. This is taking place *in the jungle, the mighty jungle.*
   a. Let There Be Drums/Sandy Nelson
   b. Young Love/Tab Hunter
   c. The Lion Sleeps Tonight/Tokens

16. He doesn't believe her because *no one could look as good as* her.
    a. Runaround Sue/Dion
    b. Oh, Pretty Woman/Roy Orbison
    c. Next Door to an Angel/Neil Sedaka

****

17. Something's missing when they're Twistin'— *let's start kissin'* to this.
    a. The Wah-Watusi/Orlons
    b. The Cha Cha Cha/Bobby Rydell
    c. Slow Twistin'/Chubby Checker

****

18. You hear them *moaning their lives away.*
    a. Lover Please/Clyde McPhatter
    b. Two Lovers/Mary Wells
    c. Chain Gang/Sam Cooke

****

19. *How does it feel being on the outside looking in?*
    a. Love Letters (Straight From Your Heart)/Ketty Lester
    b. Only Love Can Break a Heart/Gene Pitney
    c. What's A-Matter Baby/Timi Yuro

****

20. There goes their baby with someone new — *goodbye to romance that might have been.*
    a. There Goes My Baby/Drifters
    b. Tears on My Pillow/Little Anthony & the Imperials
    c. Bye Bye Love/Everly Brothers

HARDER QUESTIONS: Worth 2 points each — 4 points if you can NAME THAT TUNE without the three choices !

****

1. *If you don't like the job, put the bucket down.*
   a. Get a Job/Silhouettes
   b. Don't Let the Rain Come Down/Serendipity Singers
   c. Mule Skinner Blues/Fendermen

****

2. He has *heartache on heartache* because he finds he *can't get over losing you.*
   a. Can't Get Used to Losing You/Andy Williams
   b. Blue on Blue/Bobby Vinton
   c. Heartaches By the Number/Guy Mitchell

****

3. He can still hear *the jukebox softly playing,* thinking about what he and you used to do.
   a. Things/Bobby Darin
   b. You're The Reason/Bobby Edwards
   c. Little Boy Sad/Johnny Burnette

****

4. *From the rear a voice was heard, a brave young man with a trembling word* that rang loud and clear: *"What am I doing here?"*
   a. North to Alaska/Johnny Horton
   b. Stranded In the Jungle/Cadets
   c. Mr. Custer/Larry Verne

****

5. *Someday when* they're *as old as you,* they'll *take you and make* their *dreams come true.*
   a. Oh Julie/Crescendos
   b. Terry/Leigh Bell & the Chimes
   c. Forever/Little Dippers

ANSWERS

****

1. c. Walk Right Back/Everly Brothers
2. b. Wolverton Mountain/Claude King
3. a. Kisses Sweeter Than Wine/Jimmie Rodgers
4. b. Susie Darlin'/Robin Luke
5. a. Foolish Little Girl/Shirelles
6. a. Sheila/Tommy Roe
7. b. Image of a Girl/Safaris
8. c. Heat Wave/Martha & the Vandellas
9. a. Angel Baby/Rosie & the Originals
10. b. No Particular Place to Go/Chuck Berry
11. b. Maybe I Know/Lesley Gore
12. c. The Peppermint Twist/Joey Dee & the Starliters
13. b. Venus In Blue Jeans/Jimmy Clanton
14. a. Blame It On the Bossa Nova/Eydie Gorme
15. c. The Lion Sleeps Tonight/Tokens
16. b. Oh, Pretty Woman/Roy Orbison
17. b. The Cha Cha Cha/Bobby Rydell
18. c. Chain Gang/Sam Cooke
19. c. What's A-Matter Baby/Timi Yuro
20. c. Bye Bye Love/Everly Brothers

****

HARDER QUESTIONS--Answers

1. c. Mule Skinner Blues/Fendermen
2. b. Blue on Blue/Bobby Vinton
3. a. Things/Bobby Darin
4. c. Mr. Custer/Larry Verne
5. a. Oh Julie/Crescendos

1. *No one knows what happened that day — how his car overturned in flames.*
   - a. Dead Man's Curve/Jan & Dean
   - b. Tell Laura I Love Her/Ray Peterson
   - c. Leader of the Pack/Shangri-Las

****

2. *You're* their *first cup of coffee,* their *last cup of tea.*
   - a. You're So Fine/Falcons
   - b. The Way You Look Tonight/Lettermen
   - c. Baby (You Got What It Takes)/Brook Benton & Dinah Washington

****

3. *A little trick with Nick.*
   - a. Loop De Loop/Johnny Thunder
   - b. Loddy Lo/Chubby Checker
   - c. The Name Game/Shirley Ellis

****

4. If you tell him you're his one girl, *you'll make* his *whole life worth living just by giving your love to* him.
   - a. A Million to One/Jimmy Charles
   - b. Unchain My Heart/Ray Charles
   - c. Young World/Rick Nelson

****

5. *You don't live in a beautiful place and you don't dress in the best of taste, and nature didn't give you such a beautiful face.*
   - a. She's Not You/Elvis Presley
   - b. You Got What It Takes/Marv Johnson
   - c. Rag Doll/Four Seasons

6. *Maybe tomorrow a new romance—no more sorrow, but that's the chance you've got to take if your lonely heart breaks.*
   - a. Only the Lonely/Roy Orbison
   - b. Once In a While/Chimes
   - c. Heartaches/Marcels

****

7. When you say you love them, it's *a crazy feelin' that's got* them *reelin'.*
   - a. Rave On/Buddy Holly & the Crickets
   - b. So Fine/Fiestas
   - c. Shake, Rattle & Roll/Bill Haley & His Comets

****

8. People say that you're *a runaround lover.*
   - a. The Night Has a Thousand Eyes/Bobby Vee
   - b. You Beat Me To the Punch/Mary Wells
   - c. You'll Lose a Good Thing/Barbara Lynn

****

9. He says to *come back tomorrow night and try it again.*
   - a. Love Me/Elvis Presley
   - b. Keep a Knockin'/Little Richard
   - c. Don't Forbid Me/Pat Boone

****

10. *He's never dreaming of you — he'll break your heart, you wait and see.*
    - a. Tell Him No/Travis & Bob
    - b. Don't Bet Money Honey/Linda Scott
    - c. Forget Him/Bobby Rydell

11. They've *waited so long for your kisses and your love* — please come to them *from up above.*
    a. Little Darlin'/Diamonds
    b. Come Softly To Me/Fleetwoods
    c. My Prayer/Platters

****

12. When they were *a little bitty baby,* their mama would *rock* them *in the cradle.*
    a. Baby Blue/Echoes
    b. That's Old Fashioned/Everly Brothers
    c. Cotton Fields/Highwaymen

****

13. They wonder whether the stars are out tonight — they *don't know if it's cloudy or bright.*
    a. A Thousand Stars/Kathy Young & The Innocents
    b. I Only Have Eyes For You/Flamingos
    c. In the Still of the Night/Five Satins

****

14. He says that *only you can tame* his *heart* and *only you can tear it apart.*
    a. Tiger/Fabian
    b. Only Love Can Break a Heart/Gene Pitney
    c. Diana/Paul Anka

****

15. They found *the dance was out-a-sight the way the Lion Sleeps Tonight.*
    a. Mashed Potato Time/Dee Dee Sharp
    b. The Lion Sleeps Tonight/Tokens
    c. Loco-Motion/Little Eva

16. He'll never know *the reason why you love* him *as*
   you do.
   - a. Why/Frankie Avalon
   - b. A Wonder Like You/Rick Nelson
   - c. The Wonder of You/Ray Peterson

****

17. *True love means planning our life for two, being*
   together the whole day through.
   - a. Look In My Eyes/Chantels
   - b. I Understand (Just How You Feel)/G-Clefs
   - c. Hey Paula/Paul & Paula

****

18. *In 1814 they took a little trip.*
   - a. Time Machine/Dante & the Evergreens
   - b. The Battle of New Orleans/Johnny Horton
   - c. Over the Mountain, Across the Sea/Johnnie & Joe

****

19. *My mother told me if I was good that she would*
   buy me a rubber dolly; my auntie told her I kissed
   a soldier — now she won't buy me a rubber dolly.
   - a. Soldier Boy/Shirelles
   - b. The Clapping Song/Shirley Ellis
   - c. I'm Blue (the Gong-Gong Song)/Ikettes

****

20. She thought she was dreaming, but she was
   wrong — now she's *gonna keep on schemin'* until
   she makes you her own.
   - a. Just One Look/Doris Troy
   - b. Mama Didn't Lie/Jan Bradley
   - c. The One Who Really Loves You/Mary Wells

HARDER QUESTIONS: Worth 2 points each — 4 points if you can NAME THAT TUNE without the three choices !

****

1. The big dinosaur was a long tall lizard — he'd drift through the jungle like a slow blizzard *until he got a double-take of lady lizard.*

    a. Ape Call/Nervous Norvus
    b. Alley-Oop/Hollywood Argyles
    c. Puff The Magic Dragon/Peter Paul & Mary

****

2. *The music begins to play*, and then *automatically you're on your way.*

    a. Pony Time/Chubby Checker
    b. Mashed Potato Time/Dee Dee Sharp
    c. The Monkey Time/Major Lance

****

3. Her boyfriend and her best friend sat down right in front of her.

    a. Break It To Me Gently/Brenda Lee
    b. In My Little Corner of the World/Anita Bryant
    c. Sad Movies (Make Me Cry)/Sue Thompson

****

4. Each night he kneels and says a prayer — you and he have a love *that's sure to be true love for all eternity.*

    a. Love You So/Ron Holden
    b. Wonderful World/Sam Cooke
    c. Stairway to Heaven/Neil Sedaka

****

5. *He was panther quick and leather tough* because he *figured that he'd been pushed enough.*

    a. Killer Joe/Rockyfellers
    b. The Rebel/Johnny Cash
    c. Big Bad John/Jimmy Dean

ANSWERS

****

1. b. Tell Laura I Love Her/Ray Peterson
2. a. You're So Fine/Falcons
3. c. The Name Game/Shirley Ellis
4. c. Young World/Rick Nelson
5. b. You Got What It Takes/Marv Johnson
6. a. Only the Lonely/Roy Orbison
7. a. Rave On/Buddy Holly & the Crickets
8. a. The Night Has a Thousand Eyes/Bobby Vee
9. b. Keep a Knockin'/Little Richard
10. c. Forget Him/Bobby Rydell
11. b. Come Softly To Me/Fleetwoods
12. c. Cotton Fields/Highwaymen
13. b. I Only Have Eyes For You/Flamingos
14. c. Diana/Paul Anka
15. a. Mashed Potato Time/Dee Dee Sharp
16. c. The Wonder of You/Ray Peterson
17. c. Hey Paula/Paul & Paula
18. b. The Battle of New Orleans/Johnny Horton
19. b. The Clapping Song/Shirley Ellis
20. a. Just One Look/Doris Troy

****

HARDER QUESTIONS--Answers

1. a. Ape Call/Nervous Norvus
2. c. The Monkey Time/Major Lance
3. c. Sad Movies (Make Me Cry)/Sue Thompson
4. a. Love You So/Ron Holden
5. b. The Rebel/Johnny Cash

1. Although he told his friends that you and he would never part, his friends *laughed and said that you would break* his *heart.*
   - a. I Wonder Why/Dion & the Belmonts
   - b. Stood Up/Ricky Nelson
   - c. Oh Lonesome Me/Don Gibson

****

2. He wants you to *play your didgeridoo* until he *shoots through.*
   - a. My Boomerang Won't Come Back/Charlie Drake
   - b. Tie Me Kangaroo Down, Sport/Rolf Harris
   - c. Born Free/Matt Monro

****

3. *The ghouls all came from their humble abodes to get a jolt from* his *electrodes.*
   - a. Dinner With Drac/John Zacherle
   - b. Monster Mash/Bobby "Boris" Pickett
   - c. The Flying Saucer/Buchanan & Goodman

****

4. It *tastes real good, but it's so hard to chew.*
   - a. Sweets For My Sweet/Drifters
   - b. Peanut Butter/Coasters
   - c. Hot Pastrami/Dartells

****

5. It's the *hippest street in town.*
   - a. Washington Square/Village Stompers
   - b. Mecca/Gene Pitney
   - c. South Street/Orlons

6. They stroll by the sea together, under stars twinkling high above — *no one else but me and you.*
    a. Deep Purple/Nino Tempo & April Stevens
    b. My Summer Love/Ruby & the Romantics
    c. So Much In Love/Tymes

****

7. *Don't try to change* her *in any way* — and don't tie her down, because she *wouldn't stay.*
    a. You Don't Own Me/Lesley Gore
    b. I Will Follow Him/Little Peggy March
    c. Patches/Dickey Lee

****

8. He advises that, even *if your friends say you have no taste, go ahead and marry anyway.*
    a. If You Wanna Be Happy/Jimmy Soul
    b. You Can Have Her/Roy Hamilton
    c. You Got What It Takes/Marv Johnson

****

9. He loves *the girl with sunlight in her hair.*
    a. Kissin' Time/Bobby Rydell
    b. Lavender-Blue/Sammy Turner
    c. Venus/Frankie Avalon

****

10. He needs *somebody to be* his *baby,* someone he can *tell* his *troubles to.*
    a. Fortune Teller/Bobby Curtola
    b. A Teenage Idol/Ricky Nelson
    c. The Gypsy Cried/Lou Christie

11. They *sure like girls — from Annie to Veronica.*
   a. California Sun/Rivieras
   b. Alvin's Harmonica/Chipmunks
   c. Shout (Part 1)/Joey Dee & the Starliters

****

12. The night they met you they knew they *needed you so* — and if they had the chance, they'd *never let you go.*
   a. One Fine Day/Chiffons
   b. Be My Baby/Ronettes
   c. Honolulu Lulu/Jan & Dean

****

13. *Tequila.*
   a. Purple People Eater/Sheb Wooley
   b. Transfusion/Nervous Norvus
   c. Witch Doctor/David Seville

****

14. If you always want him to be by your side, *take his hand and swallow your foolish pride.*
   a. Foolish Little Girl/Shirelles
   b. Shoop Shoop Song (It's In His Kiss)/Betty Everett
   c. Tell Him/Exciters

****

15. When Freddy cuts in to dance, *you never speak — why must you be so meek?*
   a. You'll Lose a Good Thing/Barbara Lynn
   b. Johnny Get Angry/Joanie Sommers
   c. Hurt/Timi Yuro

16. Do this *like we did last summer — like we did last year.*
   - a. Let's Twist Again/Chubby Checker
   - b. Good Times/Sam Cooke
   - c. Baby Workout/Jackie Wilson

****

17. *Summer's here and the time is right.*
   - a. You Can't Sit Down/Dovells
   - b. Last Chance to Turn Around/Gene Pitney
   - c. Dancing In the Street/Martha & the Vandellas

****

18. Then one day he took them home *to meet his mom and his dad.*
   - a. Then He Kissed Me/Crystals
   - b. My Boyfriend's Back/Angels
   - c. Easier Said Than Done/Essex

****

19. She says that they're *doing the Twist, the Fish, the Mashed Potato, too,* and she wants to go.
   - a. Gravy (For My Mashed Potatoes)/Dee Dee Sharp
   - b. Where the Boys Are/Connie Francis
   - c. Party Lights/Claudine Clark

****

20. He got himself *a job on the railroad — the work is hard and long —* but he's going to build up a future and *show your daddy he's wrong.*
   - a. Poor Man's Son/Reflections
   - b. Midnight Mary/Joey Powers
   - c. Down In the Boondocks/Billy Joe Royal

HARDER QUESTIONS: Worth 2 points each — 4 points if you can NAME THAT TUNE without the three choices !

****

1. *She's not in love with* them.
> a. Gloria/Passions
> b. Denise/Randy & the Rainbows
> c. Mother-in-Law/Ernie K-Doe

****

2. He wants you to come — *just say you will.*
> a. Are You Really Mine/Jimmie Rodgers
> b. Lonely Teardrops/Jackie Wilson
> c. Sugar Moon/Pat Boone

****

3. *The touch of her hand captured* his *soul, and the kiss from her lips set* his *heart aglow.*
> a. My Special Angel/Bobby Helms
> b. My True Love/Jack Scott
> c. (Marie's the Name of) His Latest Flame/Elvis Presley

****

4. He closes his eyes, *softly says a thousand prayers,* and *drifts away into the magic night.*
> a. Sway/Bobby Rydell
> b. Cradle of Love/Johnny Preston
> c. In Dreams/Roy Orbison

****

5. There are *no broken hearts for* them *because* they *love each other,* and with their *faith and trust, there could be no other.*
> a. Why/Frankie Avalon
> b. Every Beat of My Heart/Gladys Knight & the Pips
> c. Portrait of My Love/Steve Lawrence

ANSWERS

****

1. a. I Wonder Why/Dion & the Belmonts
2. b. Tie Me Kangaroo Down, Sport/Rolf Harris
3. b. Monster Mash/Bobby "Boris" Pickett
4. b. Peanut Butter/Coasters
5. c. South Street/Orlons
6. c. So Much In Love/Tymes
7. a. You Don't Own Me/Lesley Gore
8. a. If You Wanna Be Happy/Jimmy Soul
9. c. Venus/Frankie Avalon
10. b. A Teenage Idol/Ricky Nelson
11. b. Alvin's Harmonica/Chipmunks
12. b. Be My Baby/Ronettes
13. a. Purple People Eater/Sheb Wooley
14. c. Tell Him/Exciters
15. b. Johnny Get Angry/Joanie Sommers
16. a. Let's Twist Again/Chubby Checker
17. c. Dancing In the Street/Martha & the Vandellas
18. a. Then He Kissed Me/Crystals
19. c. Party Lights/Claudine Clark
20. b. Midnight Mary/Joey Powers

****

HARDER QUESTIONS--Answers

1. a. Gloria/Passions
2. b. Lonely Teardrops/Jackie Wilson
3. b. My True Love/Jack Scott
4. c. In Dreams/Roy Orbison
5. a. Why/Frankie Avalon

1. Since all his life he's *been waiting, tonight there'll be no hesitating.*
    a. Let the Little Girl Dance/Billy Bland
    b. Oh Boy!/Buddy Holly & the Crickets
    c. Bring It On Home to Me/Sam Cooke

****

2. They *don't have fond desires, and* they *don't have happy hours* — they *don't have anything.*
    a. Problems/Everly Brothers
    b. Since I Don't Have You/Skyliners
    c. Tears on My Pillow/Little Anthony & the Imperials

****

3. *He said he wanted to settle down and let* her *be his girl, but first he had to do a little traveling around and see the whole wide world.*
    a. The Wanderer/Dion
    b. Soldier Boy/Shirelles
    c. Navy Blue/Diane Renay

****

4. *My darling,* he loves you and he always will.
    a. Love Me Tender/Elvis Presley
    b. I'm Stickin' With You/Jimmy Bowen
    c. Butterfly/Charlie Grace

****

5. He's *got to get to rocking* and to *boogie woogie like a knife in the back,* and he wants you to be his guest *because you've got nothing to lose.*
    a. Beyong the Sea/Bobby Darin
    b. Sea Cruise/Frankie Ford
    c. Don't Let Go/Roy Hamilton

6. *Nothing can stop* him.
   a. Duke of Earl/Gene Chandler
   b. I'm Walkin'/Fats Domino
   c. I Walk the Line/Johnny Cash

****

7. *It's easier than learning your ABC's.*
   a. The Loco-Motion/Little Eva
   b. Tossin' & Turnin'/Bobby Lewis
   c. Let's Dance/Chris Montez

****

8. *She don't cook mashed potatoes and she don't cook t-bone steaks.*
   a. Peanut Butter/Coasters
   b. Bread and Butter/Newbeats
   c. Cherry Pie/Skip & Flip

****

9. *A wave out on the ocean could never move that way.*
   a. Good Timin'/Jimmy Jones
   b. Sea of Love/Phil Phillips
   c. Poetry In Motion/Johnny Tillotson

****

10. The *camp is very entertaining, and they say* he'll *have some fun if it stops raining.*
    a. Rain Rain Go Away/Bobby Vinton
    b. Hello Muddah, Hello Fadduh/Allan Sherman
    c. From a Jack to a King/Ned Miller

11. He'll always be her *true love from now until forever* — and nothing can keep him from her, because *he is my destiny.*
    a. I Will Follow Him/Little Peggy March
    b. Frankie/Connie Francis
    c. Norman/Sue Thompson

****

12. *He'll send you flowers and* then *paint the town with another girl.*
    a. Wooden Heart/Joe Dowell
    b. You Don't Know What You've Got (Until You Lose It)/Ral Donner
    c. Sweet Talkin' Guy/Chiffons

****

13. *People say that love's a game, a game you just can't win,* but *if there's a way,* he'll *find it someday.*
    a. Put Your Head On My Shoulder/Paul Anka
    b. I'm Gonna Get Married/Lloyd Price
    c. Love Is All We Need/Tommy Edwards

****

14. They *can't get across to the other side.*
    a. Over the Mountain, Across the Sea/Johnnie & Joe
    b. Under the Boardwalk/Drifters
    c. The Mountain's High/Dick & DeeDee

****

15. *Tomorrow will be too late* because his *love won't wait.*
    a. Go Jimmy Go/Jimmy Clanton
    b. It's Now or Never/Elvis Presley
    c. Just Ask Your Heart/Frankie Avalon

16. When he was sixteen he ran away and found himself *all alone, on the stray.*
    - a. Lonely Teenager/Dion
    - b. Handy Man/Jimmy Jones
    - c. Gotta Travel On/Billy Grammer

****

17. They *met him on a Monday* — somebody told them *that his name was Bill.*
    - a. Da Doo Ron Ron/Crystals
    - b. Don't Mess With Bill/Marvelettes
    - c. He's The Kind of Boy You Can't Forget/Raindrops

****

18. Although his tears *fell like rain,* he adds that *you're the one to blame.*
    - a. Love Letters In the Sand/Pat Boone
    - b. Stood Up/Ricky Nelson
    - c. Ain't That a Shame/Fats Domino

****

19. *You can make* his *dreams come true.*
    - a. Dreamin'/Johnny Burnette
    - b. Dream Lover/Bobby Darin
    - c. Dream Baby/Roy Orbison

****

20. You even worry his pet.
    - a. Footsteps/Steve Lawrence
    - b. Puppy Love/Paul Anka
    - c. You Talk Too Much/Joe Jones

HARDER QUESTIONS: Worth 2 points each — 4 points if you can NAME THAT TUNE without the three choices !

****

1. *What would people say, what would people do, what would people think if people knew* he *was with you.*
   - a. I'm Gonna Knock on Your Door/Eddie Hodges
   - b. Makin' Love/Floyd Robinson
   - c. Diana/Paul Anka

****

2. *A rich man, a poor man, a beggar — no matter whoever you are — there's a friend waiting to guide you.*
   - a. The Enchanted Sea/Islanders
   - b. Rainbow/Russ Hamilton
   - c. Look For a Star/Gary Mills

****

3. *A strange force drew* him *to the graveyard,* where he saw his sweater *lying there upon her grave.*
   - a. Haunted House/Gene Simmons
   - b. Last Kiss/J. Frank Wilson
   - c. Laurie (Strange Things Happen)/Dickey Lee

****

4. *Old barnyard drivers are found in two classes: blind crowding hogs and speeding jackasses —* so *remember to slow down today.*
   - a. The Fool/Sanford Clark
   - b. Transfusion/Nervous Norvus
   - c. Rock Island Line/Lonnie Donegan

****

5. *Hey Boo Boo !*
   - a. Yogi/Ivy Three
   - b. Mama Look a Boo Boo/Harry Belafonte
   - c. Uh! Oh! Part 2/Nutty Squirrels

ANSWERS

****

1. b. Oh Boy!/Buddy Holly & the Crickets
2. b. Since I Don't Have You/Skyliners
3. c. Navy Blue/Diane Renay
4. a. Love Me Tender/Elvis Presley
5. b. Sea Cruise/Frankie Ford
6. a. Duke of Earl/Gene Chandler
7. a. The Loco-Motion/Little Eva
8. b. Bread and Butter/Newbeats
9. c. Poetry In Motion/Johnny Tillotson
10. b. Hello Muddah, Hello Fadduh/Allan Sherman
11. a. I Will Follow Him/Little Peggy March
12. c. Sweet Talkin' Guy/Chiffons
13. a. Put Your Head On My Shoulder/Paul Anka
14. c. The Mountain's High/Dick & DeeDee
15. b. It's Now or Never/Elvis Presley
16. a. Lonely Teenager/Dion
17. a. Da Doo Ron Ron/Crystals
18. c. Ain't That a Shame/Fats Domino
19. c. Dream Baby/Roy Orbison
20. c. You Talk Too Much/Joe Jones

****

HARDER QUESTIONS--Answers

1. b. Makin' Love/Floyd Robinson
2. c. Look For a Star/Gary Mills
3. c. Laurie (Strange Things Happen)/Dickey Lee
4. b. Transfusion/Nervous Norvus
5. a. Yogi/Ivy Three

1. Since they're not together with you, they *look for stormy weather to hide the tears* they *hope you'll never see.*
   a. Why Do Lovers Break Each Other's Heart/Bob B. Soxx & the Blue Jeans
   b. Please Love Me Forever/Cathy Jean & the Roommates
   c. Crying In the Rain/Everly Brothers

****

2. After you *take out the papers and the trash,* they want you to *bring in the dog and put out the cat.*
   a. Get a Job/Silhouettes
   b. Yakety Yak/Coasters
   c. Love Is Strange/Mickey & Sylvia

****

3. *When he says dip-di-di di-di di-di,* you know he means it from the bottom of his *boogity boogity boogity shoes.*
   a. Who Put the Bomp/Barry Mann
   b. Baby Sittin' Boogie/Buzz Clifford
   c. I'm Ready/Fats Domino

****

4. *Can you come out tonight ?*
   a. Norman/Sue Thompson
   b. Hey! Baby/Bruce Channel
   c. Sherry/Four Seasons

****

5. The smile you are smiling *you were smiling then.*
   a. Diane/Bachelors
   b. Where or When/Dion & the Belmonts
   c. Those Lazy-Hazy-Crazy Days of Summer/Nat King Cole

6. He's been told that if you do the twist, *you'll never grow old.*
  - a. The Twist/Chubby Checker
  - b. Dear Lady Twist/Gary U.S. Bonds
  - c. Twistin' the Night Away/Sam Cooke

****

7. She'll *climb to the highest steeple* and tell the world he's hers.
  - a. O Dio Mio/Annette
  - b. Broken-Hearted Melody/Sarah Vaughan
  - c. Where the Boys Are/Connie Francis

****

8. *Don't be shy, just take your time* because they'd *like to get to know you.*
  - a. Beechwood 4-5789/Marvelettes
  - b. People Say/Dixie Cups
  - c. He's So Fine/Chiffons

****

9. He's *just what* they've *dreamed about — yes, he's the boy that* they *love.*
  - a. The Boy From New York City/Ad Libs
  - b. He's Sure the Boy I Love/Crystals
  - c. Popsicles and Icicles/Murmaids

****

10. She gave him her *word of honor to be faithful,* and *you'd best be believing that* she *won't be deceiving* him.
  - a. Navy Blue/Diane Renay
  - b. Johnny Angel/Shelley Fabares
  - c. My Guy/Mary Wells

11. They told their mama on the day they were born
    not to cry when she sees that they're gone,
    because *no woman is going to settle* them *down.*
    - a. Green Green/New Christy Minstrels
    - b. Surfin' Bird/Trashmen
    - c. Gypsy Rover/Highwaymen

****

12. *Wherever you go,* their *heart will follow.*
    - a. Soldier Boy/Shirelles
    - b. When I Fall In Love/Lettermen
    - c. Dawn (Go Away)/Four Seasons

****

13. *Daddy, let your mind roll on.*
    - a. Snap Your Fingers/Joe Henderson
    - b. Chug-A-Lug/Roger Miller
    - c. Walk Right In/Rooftop Singers

****

14. They've been *made blue, lied to, turned down
    pushed around, cheated and mistreated.*
    - a. There Goes My Baby/Drifters
    - b. When Will I Be Loved/Everly Brothers
    - c. You Cheated/Shields

****

15. *Still in her teens*, she's *got plenty of rhythm and
    plenty of jive.*
    - a. Short Shorts/Royal Teens
    - b. Be-Bop Baby/Ricky Nelson
    - c. Be-Bop-A-Lula/Gene Vincent

16. They wonder if they would die *if you should ever go away.*
    - a. I Love How You Love Me/Paris Sisters
    - b. I'm Leaving It Up To You/Dale & Grace
    - c. Do I Love You/Ronettes

****

17. He was *shouting like a Southern diplomat.*
    - a. Nadine/Chuck Berry
    - b. Short Fat Fannie/Larry Williams
    - c. The Girl Can't Help It/Little Richard

****

18. He wonders how anything can survive when *little minds tear you in two.*
    - a. Conscience/James Darren
    - b. Suspicion/Terry Stafford
    - c. Town Without Pity/Gene Pitney

****

19. Right in the middle of town, they found *a paradise that's trouble-proof.*
    - a. Up On The Roof/Drifters
    - b. Chapel of Love/Dixie Cups
    - c. Sugar Shack/Jimmy Gilmer & the Fireballs

****

20. This *gives him more time to see* his *girl* and take *walks through the park beneath the shining moon* — and when they kiss, she makes his *flat-top curl.*
    - a. Primrose Lane/Jerry Wallace
    - b. Here Comes Summer/Jerry Keller
    - c. Put Your Head On My Shoulder/Paul Anka

HARDER QUESTIONS: Worth 2 points each — 4 points if you can NAME THAT TUNE without the three choices !

****

1. When you say sweet things to them, they *start trembling from head to feet.*
   - a. Da Doo Ron Ron/Crystals
   - b. Quicksand/Martha & the Vandellas
   - c. Chains/Cookies

****

2. She wants *to thank you,* though *It broke* her *heart the day* she *had to part.*
   - a. The End of the World/Skeeter Davis
   - b. Wonderful Summer/Robin Ward
   - c. We'll Sing In the Sunshine/Gale Garnett

****

3. *You're super-fine,* and he'll make sure *you're all mine.*
   - a. Good Time Baby/Bobby Rydell
   - b. Oh! Carol/Neil Sedaka
   - c. One Track Mind/Bobby Lewis

****

4. He'd give a lot of dough if only he could know the answer to his quesion — *is it "yes" or is it "no" ?*
   - a. A Lover's Question/Clyde McPhatter
   - b. Are You Lonesome Tonight/Elvis Presley
   - c. Does Your Chewing Lose Its Flavor (On the Bedpost Overnight)/Lonnie Donegan

****

5. *You stood by* him *for the whole world to see, and then* he *was ten feet tall.*
   - a. My Dad/Paul Petersen
   - b. Bless You/Tony Orlando
   - c. Sheila/Tommy Roe

ANSWERS

****

1. c. Crying In the Rain/Everly Brothers
2. b. Yakety Yak/Coasters
3. a. Who Put the Bomp/Barry Mann
4. c. Sherry/Four Seasons
5. b. Where or When/Dion & the Belmonts
6. b. Dear Lady Twist/Gary U.S. Bonds
7. c. Where the Boys Are/Connie Francis
8. a. Beechwood 4-5789/Marvelettes
9. c. Popsicles and Icicles/Murmaids
10. c. My Guy/Mary Wells
11. a. Green Green/New Christy Minstrels
12. a. Soldier Boy/Shirelles
13. c. Walk Right In/Rooftop Singers
14. b. When Will I Be Loved/Everly Brothers
15. b. Be-Bop Baby/Ricky Nelson
16. c. Do I Love You/Ronettes
17. a. Nadine/Chuck Berry
18. c. Town Without Pity/Gene Pitney
19. a. Up On The Roof/Drifters
20. b. Here Comes Summer/Jerry Keller

****

HARDER QUESTIONS--Answers

1. b. Quicksand/Martha & the Vandellas
2. b. Wonderful Summer/Robin Ward
3. a. Good Time Baby/Bobby Rydell
4. c. Does Your Chewing Lose Its Flavor (On the Bedpost Overnight)/Lonnie Donegan
5. b. Bless You/Tony Orlando

1. *You start the year off fine.*
   a. Wild One/Bobby Rydell
   b. Calendar Girl/Neil Sedaka
   c. Good Timin'/Jimmie Jones

****

2. *Everybody says he's lazy, but he's not when he's kissing* them.
   a. Don't Say Nothin' Bad About My Baby/Cookies
   b. Leader of the Pack/Shangri-Las
   c. He's a Rebel/Crystals

****

3. She *didn't know that love could be so cruel.*
   a. Keep Your Hands Off My Baby/Little Eva
   b. I'm Sorry/Brenda Lee
   c. Everybody's Somebody's Fool/Connie Francis

****

4. *You don't remember them,* but *they remember you.*
   a. Searchin'/Coasters
   b. Baby Blue/Echoes
   c. Tears on My Pillow/Little Anthony & the Imperials

****

5. Once he had a pretty girl — her name it doesn't matter — *she went away with another guy, now he won't even look at her.*
   a. Think Twice/Brook Benton
   b. Hats Off to Larry/Del Shannon
   c. Sally Go 'Round the Roses/Jaynetts

6. He's *got something that* she *can't resist — but he doesn't even know that* she *exists.*
   - a. Never In a Million Years/Linda Scott
   - b. The One Who Really Loves You/Mary Wells
   - c. Johnny Angel/Shelley Fabares

****

7. *From the locker to the blanket . . . from the blanket to the shore . . . from the shore to the water . . . guess there isn't any more.*
   - a. Down By the Station/Four Preps
   - b. Itsy Bitsy Teenie Weenie Yellow Polka-Dot Bikini/ Brian Hyland
   - c. Seven Little Girls Sitting In the Back Seat/Paul Evans

****

8. *Thursday is a hardworking day, and Friday* he *gets* his *pay.*
   - a. Working In the Coal Mine/Lee Dorsey
   - b. Banana Boat (Day-O)/Harry Belafonte
   - c. Blue Monday/Fats Domino

****

9. There must be a cloud in his head — *it can't be teardrops, for a man ain't supposed to cry.*
   - a. Raindrops/Dee Clark
   - b. Cryin'/Roy Orbison
   - c. Two Kinds of Teardrops/Del Shannon

****

10. When they're out together, they *seem to glow with the glow of love.*
    - a. Candy Girl/Four Seasons
    - b. You Belong to Me/Duprees
    - c. A Walking Miracle/Essex

11. Although he said *over and over* that he loved you, his friends said he's *a fool.*
    a. Poor Little Fool/Ricky Nelson
    b. Personality/Lloyd Price
    c. I'm A Fool For Loving You/Bobby Edwards

****

12. *Sometimes we'll sigh, sometime's we'll cry.*
    a. My Happiness/Connie Francis
    b. A Sweet Old Fashioned Girl/Teresa Brewer
    c. True Love Ways/Buddy Holly

****

13. If they were *a queen, they'd do anything that he asked, anything to make him* their *own.*
    a. He's So Fine/Chiffons
    b. Da Do Ron Ron/Crystals
    c. Don't Mess With Bill/Marvelettes

****

14. *He's the handsomest dream that you ever did see.*
    a. Mr. Lee/Bobbettes
    b. The Duke of Earl/Gene Chandler
    c. Reverend Mr. Black/Kingston Trio

****

15. He said, *"c'mon baby, it's hot in here and oh so cool outside — and if you lend me a dollar I can buy some gas and we can go for a little ride,"* to which she said to *"keep on dancing or I'll find myself another cat".*
    a. Pride and Joy/Marvin Gaye
    b. Bossa Nova Baby/Elvis Presley
    c. The "In" Crowd/Dobie Gray

16. They wish they *might make this wish come true tonight.*

    a. Sugartime/McGuire Sisters
    b. Wear My Ring/Gene Vincent & His Blue Caps
    c. Little Star/Elegants

****

17. He *had a girl,* but since she left him, he's *never been the same* — and he wonders where can she be.

    a. Donna/Ritchie Valens
    b. Lonesome Town/Ricky Nelson
    c. Lonely Street/Andy Williams

****

18. He had to leave a little girl behind *in Kingston town.*

    a. White Silver Sands/Don Rondo
    b. Little Bitty Pretty One/Thurston Harris
    c. Jamaica Farewell/Harry Belafonte

****

19. *Tell Tchaikovsky the news.*

    a. Queen of the Hop/Bobby Darin
    b. Rock & Roll Is Here to Stay/Danny & the Juniors
    c. Roll Over Beethoven/Chuck Berry

****

20. He asks what he would do if the other guy *came back and wanted you.*

    a. Secretly/Jimmie Rodgers
    b. Running Scared/Roy Orbison
    c. Stranger In Town/Del Shannon

HARDER QUESTIONS: Worth 2 points each — 4 points if you can NAME THAT TUNE without the three choices !

****

1. If they *find peace of mind* here, there's a *hope in* their *heart that you'll soon be with* them.
   - a. The Sand and the Sea/Duprees
   - b. Up On the Roof/Drifters
   - c. Cotton Fields/Highwaymen

****

2. Fatima was *eating on a raisin and a grape and an apricot and a pomegranate, a bowl of chitterlings, two bananas, three Hershey bars and sipping on an RC Cola.*
   - a. Ahab, the Arab/Ray Stevens
   - b. Little Egypt/Coasters
   - c. Popeye (the Hitchhiker)/Chubby Checker

****

3. *There's nothing in this wide world left for* them *to see.*
   - a. Stay/Maurice Williams & the Zodiacs
   - b. For Your Precious Love/Jerry Butler & the Impressions
   - c. Greenfields/Brothers Four

****

4. *Last summer beneath this tree* their love said she'd come back to them.
   - a. The Way You Look Tonight/Lettermen
   - b. The Last Leaf/Cascades
   - c. There's a Moon Out Tonight/Capris

****

5. He would beg and steal *just to feel your heart beating close to* his.
   - a. You're the Reason I'm Living/Bobby Darin
   - b. Feel So Fine/Johnny Preston
   - c. Love Me/Elvis Presley

ANSWERS

****

1. b. Calendar Girl/Neil Sedaka
2. a. Don't Say Nothin' Bad About My Baby/Cookies
3. b. I'm Sorry/Brenda Lee
4. c. Tears on My Pillow/Little Anthony & the Imperials
5. b. Hats Off to Larry/Del Shannon
6. c. Johnny Angel/Shelley Fabares
7. b. Itsy Bitsy Teenie Weenie Yellow Polka-Dot Bikini/Brian Hyland
8. c. Blue Monday/Fats Domino
9. a. Raindrops/Dee Clark
10. a. Candy Girl/Four Seasons
11. b. Personality/Lloyd Price
12. c. True Love Ways/Buddy Holly
13. a. He's So Fine/Chiffons
14. a. Mr. Lee/Bobbettes
15. b. Bossa Nova Baby/Elvis Presley
16. c. Little Star/Elegants
17. a. Donna/Ritchie Valens
18. c. Jamaica Farewell/Harry Belafonte
19. c. Roll Over Beethoven/Chuck Berry
20. b. Running Scared/Roy Orbison

****

HARDER QUESTIONS--Answers

1. a. The Sand and the Sea/Duprees
2. a. Ahab, the Arab/Ray Stevens
3. c. Greenfields/Brothers Four
4. b. The Last Leaf/Cascades
5. c. Love Me/Elvis Presley

1. *They said you were high-classed, but that was just a lie.*
   - a. Raunchy/Bill Justis
   - b. Hound Dog/Elvis Presley
   - c. Dungaree Doll/Eddie Fisher

****

2. She *will never love you—the cost of love's too dear.*
   - a. We'll Sing In the Sunshine/Gale Garnett
   - b. Kiss Me Sailor/Diane Renay
   - c. Hello Stranger/Barbara Lewis

****

3. It's the *craziest sound* they've ever heard, but they *can't understand a single word.*
   - a. Bongo Stomp/Little Joey & the Flips
   - b. Surfin' Bird/Trashmen
   - c. Papa-Oom-Mow-Mow/Rivingtons

****

4. Here *the neon lights are bright* and *there's always magic in the air.*
   - a. 500 Miles Away From Home/Bobby Bare
   - b. On Top of Spaghetti/Tom Glazer & the Do-Re-Mi Children's Chorus
   - c. On Broadway/Drifters

****

5. *She loves* them *come rain, come shine.*
   - a. So Fine/Fiestas
   - b. Love Potion Number Nine/Clovers
   - c. (You've Got) The Magic Touch/Platters

6. You *left* her *at the record hop* and said you were *going out for a soda pop.*
   - a. I Want to Be Wanted/Brenda Lee
   - b. Lipstick on Your Collar/Connie Francis
   - c. Hurt/Timi Yuro

****

7. He's *been watching you grow.*
   - a. Spanish Harlem/Ben E. King
   - b. Dream Lover/Bobby Darin
   - c. Little Bitty Pretty One/Thurston Harris

****

8. Once he was downhearted — disappointment was his closest friend — *but then you came and it soon departed* and has *never shown its face again.*
   - a. Sunny/Bobby Hebb
   - b. Hello, Dolly!/Louis Armstrong
   - c. Higher and Higher/Jackie Wilson

****

9. *How low can you go.*
   - a. Limbo Rock/Chubby Checker
   - b. Twist, Twist Senora/Gary U.S. Bonds
   - c. The Stroll/Diamonds

****

10. *When the rooster crows at the break of dawn,* they'll be gone.
   - a. I Can Never Go Home Anymore/Shangri-Las
   - b. Don't Think Twice (It's Alright)/Peter, Paul & Mary
   - c. Deep Purple/Nino Tempo & April Stevens

11. They wonder if this is *a lasting treasure or just a moment's pleasure.*

      a. Will You Love Me Tomorrow/Shirelles

      b. Heat Wave/Martha & the Vandellas

      c. Save the Last Dance For Me/Drifters

****

12. One of these days, a girl *who knows all about him will break his very heart.*

      a. You Beat Me To the Punch/Mary Wells

      b. The Cheater/Bob Kuban & the In-Men

      c. Selfish One/Jackie Ross

****

13. *Walking through the park, it wasn't quite dark,* he saw *a man sitting on a bench,* moaning something that *made no sense.*

      a. Sukiyaki/Kyu Sakamoto

      b. Danke Shoen/Wayne Newton

      c. Um, Um, Um, Um, Um, Um/Major Lance

****

14. *A smile from your lips brings the summer sunshine; the tears from your eyes bring the rain.*

      a. My Special Angel/Bobby Helms

      b. You Are My Destiny/Paul Anka

      c. Please Mr. Sun/Tommy Edwards

****

15. He wants him to draw back his bow and let his *arrow go straight into* his *lover's heart.*

      a. Cupid/Sam Cooke

      b. Mr. Custer/Larry Verne

      c. Mr. Lonely/Bobby Vinton

16. *Something's missing when they're Twisting.*
    a. Blame It On the Bossa Nova/Eydie Gorme
    b. The Peppermint Twist/Joey Dee & the Starliters
    c. The Cha-Cha-Cha/Bobby Rydell

****

17. *You would cry too if it happened to you.*
    a. Wipe Out/Surfaris
    b. It's My Party/Lesley Gore
    c. All Alone Am I/Brenda Lee

****

18. He wonders what went wrong with their love, *a love that was so strong.*
    a. Don't Play That Song (You Lied)/Ben E. King
    b. Chip Chip/Gene McDaniels
    c. Runaway/Del Shannon

****

19. *You don't realize what you do to* them, and they *didn't realize what a kiss could be.*
    a. Jennie Lee/Jan & Arnie
    b. 'Til I Kissed You/Everly Brothers
    c. So This Is Love/Castells

****

20. *Long live rock & roll!*
    a. School Day/Chuck Berry
    b. Rock Around the Clock/Bill Haley & His Comets
    c. Those Oldies But Goodies/Little Caesar & the Romans

HARDER QUESTIONS: Worth 2 points each — 4 points if you can NAME THAT TUNE without the three choices !
****

1. *Oh but he watches so sadly — how can he tell her he loves her.*
   - a. Oh Pretty Woman/Roy Orbison
   - b. Dang Me/ Roger Miller
   - c. The Girl From Ipanema/Astrud Gilberto

****

2. It went *zip when it moved and pop when it stopped and whirrrr when it stood still.*
   - a. Charms/Bobby Vee
   - b. The Marvelous Toy/Peter, Paul & Mary
   - c. Little Red Rooster/Sam Cooke

****

3. *She's* his *baby doll —* she's the woman *that gives* him *more more more.*
   - a. Peggy Sue/Buddy Holly & the Crickets
   - b. Party Doll/Buddy Knox
   - c. Be-Bop-A-Lula/Gene Vincent & His Blue Caps

****

4. Though the world is filled with wondrous things, *they wouldn't have much meaning without you.*
   - a. Wonderful! Wonderful!/Tymes
   - b. Remember Then/Earls
   - c. There's a Reason/Cascades

****

5. They're *in heaven every time* they *look at you —* and they're *so lucky because* they *found a girl like you.*
   - a. Diane/Bachelors
   - b. Denise/Randy & the Rainbows
   - c. My Own True Love/Duprees

ANSWERS

****

1. b. Hound Dog/Elvis Presley
2. a. We'll Sing In the Sunshine/Gale Garnett
3. c. Papa-Oom-Mow-Mow/Rivingtons
4. c. On Broadway/Drifters
5. a. So Fine/Fiestas
6. b. Lipstick on Your Collar/Connie Francis
7. c. Little Bitty Pretty One/Thurston Harris
8. c. Higher and Higher/Jackie Wilson
9. a. Limbo Rock/Chubby Checker
10. b. Don't Think Twice (It's Alright)/Peter, Paul & Mary
11. a. Will You Love Me Tomorrow/Shirelles
12. b. The Cheater/Bob Kuban & the In-Men
13. c. Um, Um, Um, Um, Um, Um/Major Lance
14. a. My Special Angel/Bobby Helms
15. a. Cupid/Sam Cooke
16. c. The Cha-Cha-Cha/Bobby Rydell
17. b. It's My Party/Lesley Gore
18. c. Runaway/Del Shannon
19. b. 'Til I Kissed You/Everly Brothers
20. a. School Day/Chuck Berry

****

HARDER QUESTIONS--Answers

1. c. The Girl From Ipanema/Astrud Gilberto
2. b. The Marvelous Toy/Peter, Paul & Mary
3. c. Be-Bop-A-Lula/Gene Vincent & His Blue Caps
4. a. Wonderful! Wonderful!/Tymes
5. b. Denise/Randy & the Rainbows

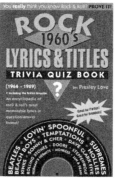

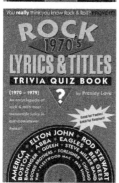

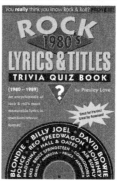

Available on Amazon.com

Printed in Great Britain
by Amazon

56618931R00078